insel taschenbuch 4762
Bett
Berlin – Fa

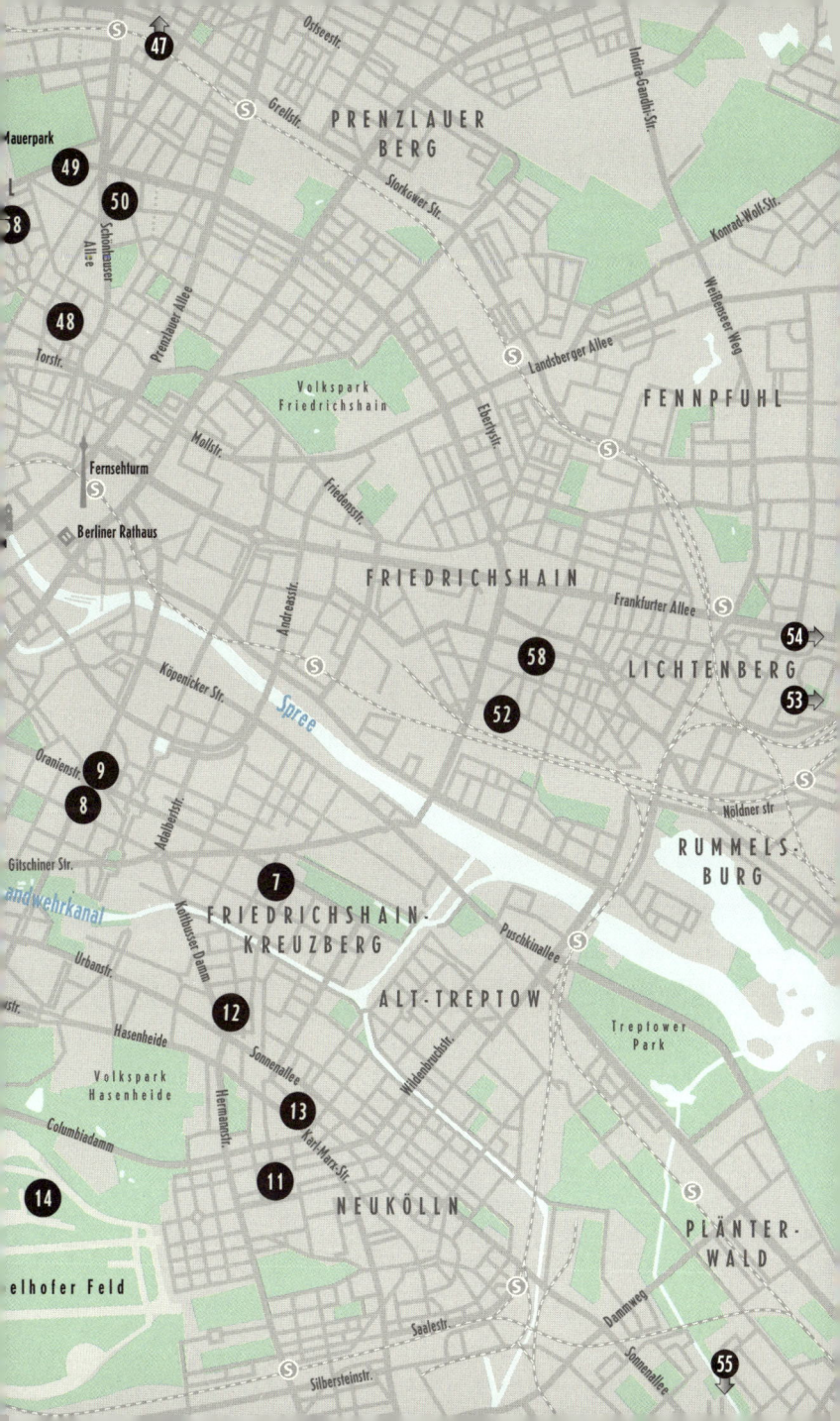

FAVOURITE PLACES

Insel

BERLIN

BETTINA RUST

WITH PHOTOGRAPHS BY THE AUTHOR

TRANSLATED BY
ALEXANDER BOOTH

✳

The original German edition *Lieblingsorte – Berlin*
was published in 2018 by Insel Verlag, Berlin.

With big thanks to
Marcus and Lucas

First edition 2019

insel taschenbuch 4763
English edition
© Insel Verlag Berlin 2019
All rights reserved.
No part of this publication may be reproduced in any form or by any means –
graphic, electronic or mechanical, including photocopying, recording, taping or
information storage and retrieval systems – without the written permission
of the publishers.
Distributed by Suhrkamp Taschenbuch Verlag
Cover and Layout: Marion Blomeyer, München
Illustration: Ryo Takemasa, Tokyo
Maps: Peter Palm, Berlin
Set: Greiner & Reichel, Köln
Printed by CPI – Ebner & Spiegel, Ulm
Printed in Germany.
ISBN 978-3-458-36463-4

TABLE OF CONTENTS

Mitte

1

Such a Beautiful City

MONBIJOU BRIDGE
BETWEEN AM KUPFERGRABEN
AND MONBIJOUSTRASSE
10117 BERLIN

Life is constant change. Hardly have you got into a groove when all of a sudden something calls for readjustment. You have to come up with new strategies, set out on new paths, employ new systems. We recognise this on a global scale, but sometimes the local changes are what really seem to turn everything upside down. Small things: a construction site, for example, right outside your door. Somehow life already feels different. For one whole year constant hammering, digging, dust whirling through the air, wobbling cranes, half-detached tarpaulins whipping angrily through windy nights, no more parking spaces, no birdsong, and not a single open window, just two Dixi-toilets out on the pavement. The small everyday changes we all have to put up with, gnashing our teeth. But what would happen if through some stupid circumstance, some twist of fate, your job ended and in order to keep working you had to move to Bad Godesberg? Of all places! Or you fell head-over-heels for someone from Papua New Guinea? This is all purely hypothetical, of course, but I've given a lot of thought to what it would take for me to turn my back on my city. Love might be the only reason. Bad Godesberg, for whatever it's worth, would never happen. And so, just like how when we're feeling down we sometimes consciously rub salt in our wounds by listening to really really sad songs that just make everything seem worse, before saying goodbye I would make my way to a place that makes my heart take flight every time, a place I can depend on, and I'd say: Berlin, you endearing city, I'm so happy I get to live here.

I'd take the Monbijou Bridge across the Spree to the Kupfergraben. Like a strong arm, the bridge touches the tip of Museum Island, which has the Pergamon Museum, the Alte Nationalgalerie, the Neues and Alte Museums, and the proud cathedral, as if it was built just to support the star-struck tourist gazing at the majestic Bode Museum with its large dome, their eyes moving left towards Alexanderplatz and then further still towards the Monbijou Theatre with its adjoining park, where in summer Berliners and tourists alike have barbeques, sit at the beach bar and look out onto the water that is constantly decorated by barges, little boats, and countless tourist steamers with names like "Mirth" or "Sanssouci", and on certain nights you can see people tango beneath colourful string lights. And further still your eyes take in the Ebert Bridge crossing Friedrichstrasse, in the direction of the Berliner Ensemble, the Friedrichstadtpalast, the Deutsches Theater. An aesthetically pleasing and lively 360-degree panorama full of variety, history, and a certain kind of elegance which, truth be told, isn't all that easy to find in Berlin, unless you're willing to make a few compromises. I wouldn't be doing myself any favours and, in the end, I'd suffer like a dog, but this is where I would say goodbye to Berlin, if I had to say goodbye to Berlin.

Over a 100 and Still Timeless

If Clärchens Ballhaus were a person, you'd want to sit next to her on the train. She could tell you some incredible stories. And I know I'm not the only one who feels that this is one of the few places where, at least tentatively, you can take a nostalgic trip to a Berlin that has nothing to do with today's. A last witness of sorts, one who went through two fins de siècle, survived two world wars and more than two systems of government. And she's still there, noble, pretty in her old get-up, surrounded by coffee shops, chic stores, and galleries. If Clärchens Ballhaus were a person, she'd be rather surprised. But she'd take it all with a sense of humour.

CLÄRCHENS BALLHAUS
AUGUSTSTRASSE 24
10117 BERLIN
OPEN DAILY FROM 11AM UNTIL END
WEEKENDS UNTIL 4AM
WWW.BALLHAUS.DE

Back in 1913, in a building constructed in 1895, husband-and-wife team Fritz and Clara Bühler opened Bühler's Ballhaus. There were close to 900 such places in Imperial Berlin, and this was one – and to get it out of the way right at the start: it's the only one where people still go to dance and have fun almost every day. With its large, ground-floor dance hall and 120-square-metre hall of mirrors, the establishment quickly found its audience. Often seen drawing at the bar, painter Heinrich Zille was a regular. As was his artist colleague Otto Dix, who designed the Ballhaus' poster, still in use today. After Fritz gave up the ghost in 1929, his fearless wife Clara, who would marry two times more, took over and continued using the same name. After the world wars, there was a notable surplus of women, so Clärchen (Clara's nickname) organised widows' balls and kept the people dancing. Even in the GDR. The Ballhaus was a meeting point for a diverse crowd from both East and West, which, naturally, did not go unnoticed. As it was taken for granted that an innocent turn on the dance floor might lead to a markedly less-than-innocent epilogue, the Stasi referred to the ballroom as the 'gonorrhoea den'. Up through 2004 the ballroom was run by the same family. Then the new owner expanded the programme and breathed new life into the first-floor hall of mirrors, which had lately been used as a storage room. This jewel is now used for events as well as for their Sunday series of classical music concerts. There is a dance tea downstairs on Sundays from 3pm to 9pm. Events are always packed. You can also find a disco Tuesday (free entry), swing nights with dance-partner placement, and various courses throughout the week (for example, Standard/Latin, West Coast Swing). And if dancing isn't quite your thing, you still have your pick of the restaurant as well as the attractive beer garden out front. Order yourself a mug of beer, gaze out at the string lights, trees, and flowers, and at the charming grey façade. Imagine what it was like a hundred years ago and allow yourself to fall out of a time for a spell.

3

Regional Delicacies

VOM EINFACHEN DAS GUTE
INVALIDENSTRASSE 155
10115 BERLIN
TEL. 030 288 64 849
TUE. - SUN. 10AM - 8PM

I first got to know former minister Renate Künast in 2009, when she was a guest on my radio show. Years later when we made plans to get together for a shoot, she suggested we meet at Invalidenstrasse 155: 'Make sure you're hungry.'

And so I found myself waiting out in front of a small shop with a table and chairs on the pavement. 'The best of the simple' was written on the window, impressively overflowing with delicious-looking bread, wine, cheese, ham, and dried sausages hanging from a line. The painterly arranged goods reminded me of drawings in old fairy-tale books of a castle banquet.

She arrived on her bicycle. Step-

ping inside, it was clear that Künast is a familiar face here. 'Hello! How nice of you to stop by.' 'Yes, I'm expecting company and wanted to pick up a few things first. And I brought someone else along.' That someone else was me, and it was absolutely amazing inside. The man behind the counter laughed. 'Where do we want to start?' Künast pointed to a brightly coloured cheese. 'Oh yes, goat cheese, mild, with honey.' We were allowed to try. We were handed a slice of sausage, then wonderfully fragrant bread. And then some ham that was so tender it melted in my mouth. 'Everything organic', Künast says. As if there was any doubt. 'Try some. They simply don't make this kind of *Leberwurst* any more.'

And that was clearly the incentive and the aspiration of the owners, who opened up shop in 2013. The two of them wanted to find and share the good things: unadulterated, natural, traditionally prepared food. Of its 45-square metres of retail space, a good portion is taken up by the counter. Toward the back there is another large table with chairs, while up on high wooden shelves oil, wine bottles, and various jars are filled with delicacies.

Our bags full (paper, naturally), we left the shop. They also do culinary evenings, with wine tastings and all the rest. It's always lovely.' The dates can be found on their website. We walked to nearby Weinbergspark and spread our delicatessen out on the lawn for our impromptu picnic. The grass was damp, but by the time we noticed, we had already sat down. Künast, the former federal minister for food, agriculture, and consumer protection, who is passionate about appropriate livestock farming, pesticide-free fertiliser, and fair trade, happily put a slice of cheese into her mouth. Ms Turbo, the warrior and true believer, sat in the afternoon sun and simply enjoyed the moment. And immediately something rather soft, almost girlish, appeared in that bright-eyed face. It suited her. Man, is this good.

Back to the Future

One of the best-kept secrets of the communications field is that there is always a lack of information. And that would be enough to make you bend over laughing if it weren't often so frustrating, its effects so serious. Both professional and personal messages are often conveyed incorrectly, unclearly, or simply not at all. And what comes out in the end is not infrequently incomplete and distorted. At this point, a knowing nod to whoever first came up with the game of Chinese Whispers: you knew it all along.

In the end, most communication issues affect all aspects of society. And it's not just the daily multitude of information that makes us inattentive, but the multitude

MUSEUM FOR COMMUNICATION BERLIN
LEIPZIGER STRASSE 16
10117 BERLIN
TEL. 030 202 940
TUE. 9AM – 8PM, WED. – FRI. 9AM – 5PM,
SAT. – SUN. 10AM – 6PM
WWW.MFK-BERLIN.DE

how you define it: unplugging from it all, everything, for two whole days (which no one does, of course); going to a silent monastery (which very few do); deactivating all your alerts and ringtones (reasonable, if not for firemen, police officers, midwives, mothers, fathers, etc.). Or you can choose the exposure-therapy method and head off for the impressive Museum for Communication, which with its exhibition pieces, explanations, and experiments may be educational, but can also be viewed as a playground. What was it like for people in the past? Who used which channels and when? Mail coach, carrier pigeon, message in a bottle, the distant ancestors of email. 'What is that?' – 'That, my dear child, is an answering machine, but yes, it looks a lot like a cassette player, ha.' 'What's a cassette player?' Or: 'There were little houses, dear, with thick books hanging in them and a handset with an earpiece ('What's an earpiece?'), you had to toss change into a slit to make a call. Not infrequently there would be a queue of people standing out in front of this little yellow box, which looked a bit like a shower stall, and they'd roll their eyes and angrily tap their feet whenever the person inside put in more money.'

of channels through which these messages arrive and in which they get caught up. Speaking of getting caught up: on top of everything there are all the classic miscommunications that thrive on the fertile ground of any old relationship like merry mushrooms in damp moss: 'But just a minute ago you thought ...', 'Why don't you say what ...', 'Hadn't we agreed that ...'

From time to time it might be helpful to come back down to earth. There's a good reason why terms like authenticity and mindfulness are enjoying a comeback (you can now even get them from the local chemist's shop as wall stickers). Coming down can help, no matter

How far away that all is now. Or two cans with a wire pulled taut between them – who still remembers? Telegrams. Signing off: a colourful image, a nasty noise, and that was that. An extensive permanent exhibition considers the past, which every day ends anew, a past that took place bit by bit for centuries but since the middle of the last one has been leaping forward at a clip. There are temporary exhibitions, performances, and special events. Generally speaking, it's fun to occupy yourself with communication, but it's also a bit humbling. Even if you don't need any of this to keep your head on straight, you will still be informed and entertained.

5

Lovely Chaos

Esteemed ladies and gentlemen, I have been eagerly following every episode of your before-and-after show in which you point your subjects to examples of their most unbecoming and incongruous outfits. Today I finally got up the nerve to ask you for help myself. In a way, with me, it's got to do with urban planning. My name is the Kulturforum. I am happy with my position and size; I'm referring more to the arrangement, the composition of all of my buildings, which causes a certain amount of confusion. I do not want to complain about the architects whatsoever. Hans Scharoun, for example, was responsible for the Philharmonie, and Mies van der

Rohe designed my Neue Nationalgalerie. All very successfully, I might add, no question. The Gemäldegalerie, the museums, and the new Staatsbibliothek (Berlin State Library) – I like them all. But they seem like an order that hasn't been picked up yet. Or consider delicate St.-Matthäus Church, which has been here since 1844; it's the only historical building left. Surrounded by her modern neighbours, she feels a bit out of place, almost like she's just been spit out of a 3D printer. And yet, she's so beautiful. Well, what do you say to a church? Come on, we've already made it through some very different times. Be a bit more patient. Perhaps you will like one of your new neighbours: a 'Museum of the Modern' for 20th-century art, for example, is just being built. Indeed! Please understand – it all may not work out. I'm running out of ideas, and this is why I am turning to you.

Oh, you poor, interesting Kulturforum. As long as no one invents an immense gripper able to lift up buildings and put them somewhere else, you will just have to live with this unique and lovely form of chaos. In spite of, or perhaps because of, its inconsistency, this is a very inspiring place; in the end, the individual institutions here keep their promises. A concert in the Philharmonie? Unique. The paintings in the Gemäldegalerie? Impressive.

The atmosphere of the area alone is special. To warm up to it all it's best to start off at Ahmed's Imbiss, right next to the Neue Nationalgalerie, which at the moment is a giant construction site. 'We've got great sandwiches, currywurst, chips. And my coffee is the real thing. It's really good coffee', he says. Who have you always wanted to serve here, Ahmed? 'Angela Merkel. She's driven by in her car before but never stepped out.' Why Angela Merkel? 'I love her. She's a bit... hmm, I don't know, strong and all.' Perhaps one day she will indeed make a stop on a nice midday in fall. The Chancellor would grab two plastic chairs and place them in the late afternoon sun, put up her legs, bite into a warm sandwich, and at long last have a cup of Ahmed's coffee. Chaos or not!

Kreuzberg

6

The Flâneur Traipses off to the Waterfall

VIKTORIAPARK
KREUZBERGSTRASSE 15
10965 BERLIN

For years I have moderated a show on Radio Eins called "Audible Rust" where I invite musicians, authors, actors, and politicians to bring their favourite songs with them. Ultimately, every one of us has their own musical photo-album of sorts: my first record, the song of my first kiss, my first flat, the song you associate with a particular holiday, plaster cast, or new job. But it's not only songs. Our brains continuously dispense colourful little pins across our interior city maps: we first met each other on this corner; I ate bad mussels at that restaurant; here they towed my car; around the corner I wanted to get a place at one point. Naturally, my Berlin is chock full of

pins, and one of them is in Kreuz-berg's Viktoriapark.

For many Berliners this park is the coolest among all the inner-city greenspaces. Most of all this has to do, of course, with the Kreuzbergers themselves, their non-conformity and general craziness long a symbol of wild Berlin. As to how wild it is today, I don't want to guess. Suffice it to say that the mix of people living there is still pretty heterogenous – despite the horrendous cost of housing. The latter has a huge influence on the former, and the 13-hectare large Viktoriapark increases this area's quality of life. Right at the park there is a laid-back beer garden, the Golgotha, opposite the w restaurant; there's a small petting zoo for kids; and, last but not least, the site that gives its name to the whole: the Kreuzberg at its heart, which in winter turns into a sledding hill. At the top of the – vertigo-inducing, for Berliners – 66-metre-tall hill, King Friedrich Wilhelm III in 1818 laid the foundation stone for an imposing neo-Gothic national monument which was to remind people of the important battles, defeats, and victories of 1813's Wars of Liberation. Topping it off is a cross that according to various sources gave the area its name.

It was only about 70 years later that they decided to build a park around it and, while they were at it, okayed the proposal for an artificial, 24-metre-high waterfall. The views across the city, particularly the northward view over the waterfall, are uplifting. And whenever I'm up here, my inner pin begins to sting me a bit, and I remember a New Year's morning many years before. While the city was busy sleeping off its New Year's hangover, I walked up the Kreuzberg with a heavy heart, past bare winter trees and the remains of fireworks. I was stuck in a messy love affair, as we all sometimes are. Encouraged by the freshness of the year, I made up my mind to rouse myself from my self-pity without delay. When I found a keychain in the form of a heart lying in the snow next to my car on my way back, I naturally took it as a sign. It couldn't be any more clear-cut! Half a year later I lost it again, but by that time I was long out of the woods. Nothing to do with magic, I know; time is an amazing healer. But maybe it really was a kind of talisman. And if so, I'd give a whole lot to know whether its mojo is still working, regardless of who it ended up with.

The First Super-market Without Packaging

Once upon a time, hotel rooms were advertised as having running water and colour TV. That was classy. There were walking and talking dolls with little plastic records you could slip in their backs, skipping ropes, naughty boys in short lederhosen, and gold-edged curtains. Snickers packets were red, taxis were black, telephone cabins yellow. Relatives were referred to as Uncle and Auntie, and out in the courtyard was a single rubbish bin, one grey rubbish bin where you tossed everything without a second thought. When I take out the trash today, I look like an octopus. I sure wish I had multiple arms, one for my keys, one to open all the doors, the others

ORIGINAL UNVERPACKT
WIENER STRASSE 16
10999 BERLIN
MON. - SAT. 11AM - 7PM
WWW.ORIGINAL-UNVERPACKT.DE

to take care of the paper, regular rubbish, glass, packaging, and organic waste. Absolute madness. Though by now I can block it out, I always feel bad when I stand in front of all the bins, as it becomes undeniably clear just how much trash each and every one of us produces every day. Separating rubbish may help the problem somewhat, but it certainly will not solve it. Isn't it a bit misleading to try and make ourselves feel better by dutifully sorting our cheese packaging, newspapers, and juice bottles and leaving it up to the recycling plants? As if they didn't need to use monstrous amounts of energy and water too.

Milena Glimbovski had a better idea. What would it be like to open a shop that only offers unpackaged and predominately organic groceries and household goods? Together with her team she came up with a concept, started a crowdfunding campaign, and in 2014 opened the first Original Unverpackt store on Wiener Strasse in Kreuzberg. Here shoppers can choose completely unpackaged groceries and then go and weigh them. The procedure is surprisingly uncomplicated and hygienic – there are tongs, gloves, and spigots. You can bring whatever tins, jars, bottles, and bags you need from home, buy them onsite, or order them from their well-organised website, which also provides more information on the whole zero-waste idea in general. There are numerous links and tips on the mantra of 'refuse, reduce, reuse, recycle'.

Not that I drive over to Kreuzberg every few days with a bag full of jars, no. But when I'm in the area, I always stop by. Their products are tasty and fresh, and the idea is without a doubt worthy of support. And even if people like Milena and ideas like Original Unverpackt are still too small to provide the death-blow to all of our wasteful rituals – once they get a foot in the door of our comfortable routines, things will already be underway.

Multi-coloured, Green, and Red Garden Plots

PRINZESSINNENGÄRTEN
PRINZENSTRASSE 35-38
10969 BERLIN
15 APRIL - OCTOBER,
DAILY FROM 10AM - 10PM
WWW.PRINZESSINNENGÄRTEN.NET

I know Addi from back when I still lived in Hannover. He was a director. Once he filmed a man walking backwards through the city. Then he played the film back normally so that the man seemed to be the only one walking forwards. In his early 20s, he moved to Berlin like so many others who were different, more imaginative, less conformist. During my holidays I would visit him, he was living in the building behind Café M. In *Zitty* magazine one day I read about a flea market at Moritzplatz, not far from the Wall. I grabbed a bicycle and rode over. The day was grey and so was the empty lot by the roundabout that the traffic was nervously circling. Dust,

stones, dried puddles. The sheets and trestle tables were full of forlorn things, linty wool tights, a few Russian fur hats, some single gloves next to dried garlic sausages. Pretty different.

Today it's hard to believe it ever looked like that. After being ignored for more than half a century, this place has become an immense and wild city garden, the wasteland vanished in a burst of green blooms and vines. Walking the small paths past the many stands and garden plots on the some 6,000-square-metre space, it seems incredible that this refuge has only existed since 2009. Local residents and engaged citizens came together to form a non-profit they named Nomad-ic Green and freed the area from two tons of rubbish. And even though the usage rights were only extended provisionally, they took action: planting garden plots, harvesting home-grown vegetables, and establishing bee colonies. They started a garden café and a restaurant. They began to sell seeds, saplings, and plants from their stands, advice included. Like with so many other unconventional projects in this city, the temporary rental agreement hangs over the Prinzessinnengärten's metaphorical head like the sword of Damocles. The land belongs to the city, and in this time of limited living space and privatisation politics, the only option open to all those connected to the project is to apply for a further extension – which might not come. We all know how important it is to protect ecological spaces for the wellbeing of all, especially when the place matches its use so well. A perfect combination. You no longer even want to imagine the one without the other; like naked feet and sand, hot pancakes and maple syrup, and Steffi Graf and André Agassi, Moritzplatz and the Prinzessinnengärten belong together.

An article in *Die Zeit* magazine once said that the Prinzessinnengärten understood itself to be a biotope as well as a sociotope, and this is probably the best description you will find. Here, bicycles are repaired, things get recycled and upcycled, hardcore eco-Kreuzbergers meet neophyte balcony-enjoying Charlottenburgers, school classes learn that sunflower seeds grow in the face of those big, yellow flowers and that the jack-o-lantern with its carved grimace is actually known as a pumpkin and can even be eaten. Here, people harvest vegetables, fix meals and give advice, drink coffee, eat, and talk. A blooming microcosm bedded down in the midst of all that loud traffic like the hole at the centre of the donut. And though this might not be the place to find stillness, it's ideal for finding peace.

9

A Temple for Creative Types and Artists

Over the course of evolutionary fine-tuning, we are increasingly turning away from the luxury of owning our own cars. This is by all means a positive thing for the environment. But it would be a real shame for the staging of any self-respecting success story: no car means no garage. Indeed, in the future we'll probably have to do without inventions completely, seeing as legend has it that so many were cooked up in garages (just think of Hewlett Packard, Google, or Microsoft, for starters). Modulor is no different: two architecture students from Berlin, brothers Christoph and Ulrich Struhk, were annoyed by the fact that the materials they needed to build their models could

MODULOR: SUPPLIES FOR ARCHITECTS
AND ARTISTS
PRINZENSTRASSE 85
10969 BERLIN
TEL. 030 690 360
MON. - FRI. 9AM - 8PM, SAT. 10AM - 6PM
WWW.MODULOR.DE / FILIALE-BERLIN

only be bought in bulk. Well then, they would just go ahead and form their own company, selling small quantities of Styrofoam, acrylic and PVC, wooden sticks and metal pipes, MDF panels, glue, and much much more. They rented a garage in a rear building in Kreuzberg in 1988, and that's where it all got started. The idea took off. Soon architectural students were no longer their only clients, and the Struhk brothers had to find a new location. In 2011 they found it in Moritzplatz' Aufbau Haus, a newly renovated industrial building that, in addition to housing the Aufbau publishing house that gives the building its name, also has a theatre, an art gallery, various ateliers, a wonderful bookstore, a club, and more.

After repeatedly expanding their range of products, this store is no longer just a mecca for professionals but for anyone who has a soft spot for paper, pens, handpicked creative literature, art books, boxes, calendars, and adhesive foil. Materials are cut upon request, and they even sell worktables and chairs. The 3,000-square-metre space expands across multiple levels and offers over 30,000 products. The concept is neither DIY-colourful nor crazy-creative, but reserved and attractive in its simplicity.

Take a bit of time and send any companion who is unresponsive to all of these objects' charms to the café directly across from the entrance. You simply won't be able to zip through this place. When you walk outside again after about 45 minutes, your thoughts moving about the Moritzplatz roundabout, you'll notice that your bag contains two soft mechanical pencils, a roll of wrapping paper decorated with a map of Berlin, some neon-yellow adhesive tape, a book about street art, and a simple metal box. You will ask yourself how you were actually able to live without all of it for so long. Or why you wanted to.

10

Café Eule in Gleisdreieck Park

CAFÉ EULE
BÜLOWSTRASSE
10963 BERLIN

MARCH - OCTOBER,
MON. - SUN. 10AM - 7.30PM
NOVEMBER - FEBRUARY,
SAT. - SUN. 12 PM - 6PM
WWW.FACEBOOK.COM / CAFEEULEIM
WESTPARK

There aren't a lot of advantages to growing older, save learning that as far as love at first sight is concerned it might be healthier to wait for a second glance. This will not *always* keep you from emotional disasters, but often enough. For me, Gleisdreieck Park was a candidate for the second chance. Located between Schöneberg, Kreuzberg, and Mitte, this 31.5-hectare park, formerly the site of a train depot for the Berlin Anhalter station and freight yard, opened in 2011. Thanks to some passionate citizen initiatives, the park, which is divided into three sections, saw some truly good ideas come into being: the garden allotments and a few railroad relics were allowed

to stay, new plots were planted, paths made, grassy spaces laid down, plus unusual seating, playgrounds, and even 25 beach-volleyball courts (Beach 21). Residents were quickly enthusiastic about this huge amount of newly green space, and a mix of generations and nationalities took to walking the freshly paved walkways past the freshly planted trees. In a flash, numerous apartments appeared at the edge of the park, grouped together in new residential areas. Of course, even then it all looked a bit imposing and incredibly New-Yorky when the yellow *U-Bahn* snaked its way across the viaducts, and the long-distance trains optically divided the east of the park

from the west. But I still couldn't quite warm to the place, it lacked a kind of patina and charm; I could still sense the drawing board where it all had been created, not grown. That is, up until the day I rode my bicycle along a shortcut through the park and discovered Café Eule on my way through the garden allotments. Café Eule was opened by Kristiana Elig, who together with her family owns a plot there. Following her father's death, she originally got the idea to open a cemetery café, one that would not be gloomy or sad, and one where she could sell her baked goods. Her search for the right place came to naught. 'Then the board of the garden allotments spoke to me and said: "Funny lady with the lovely cakes, come do that here. Open a café, you'll pay a tiny bit of rent, and we have a space where everyone can meet. People who visit the park too. Do it!" And that's how I got started.' At Café Eule you'll run into a lot of children, families, allotment folks, and passers-by who can no longer do without Kristiana's entirely homemade and exclusively vegetarian specialties. A lot of the ingredients, like the fruit, vegetables, and herbs, come directly from the garden allotment. In addition to the aforementioned cakes, Kristiana's soups, fresh lemonade, organic spelt-dough pizza, couscous, quiches, and more are incredible. All total, there are about 100 outdoor seats, while during the winter months Eule is only open on weekends. But with a brazier to keep you warm on the outside, the elderberry punch with rum-soaked raisins will definitely keep you warm on the inside.

Neukölln

Centre for Contemporary Art and More

The very first thing a budding bard must do is get used to drinking brew

–Wilhelm Busch

In 8th or 9th grade, I visited a brewery with my school. At that time, we would of course just as gladly have gone to visit a crematorium or a slaughterhouse; the important thing was just not to have any lessons. I only remember three things about this trip: the smell (bad), grown-ups with little white bonnets (funny), and a tasting that only our teacher was allowed to enjoy while we had to fidget about on the benches in the hall. The fact that after such inauspicious beginnings I would once again find myself in

KINDL – CENTRE FOR CONTEMPORARY ART
AM SUDHAUS 3
12053 BERLIN
TEL. 030 832 159 120
WED. – SUN. 12PM – 6PM

a brewery many years later at first escaped me.

I wanted to see Kindl, a new centre for contemporary art housed in the former Kindl brewery in Neukölln. Built in 1872, this imposing building of dark-red brick stands out against the bright blue sky like something from a painting. In 2005, the new Berliner-Kindl-Schultheiss Brewery opened in Weissensee, and the Neukölln brewery passed into the hands of private investors in 2009. Thankfully they did not turn the buildings into luxury lofts but turned them over to the wild wills of art. As soon as I walked in, my breath stopped. Good god, what a space, what sheer size, what architecture!

Here and there, in friendly co-existence with the massive and bizarre copper boilers, were a few tables with people sitting and eating and talking. Next to the immense boilers they looked like Playmobil figures. The former Sudhaus is now known as König Otto, which is run by Nikoletta and Tante Poppi, who serve Mediterranean, vegetarian, and vegan food. They offer a changing lunch menu, homemade cake, wine, Kindl beer, of course, and – pay attention – Rollberg beer, a quasi in-house brew from the private brewery located underneath the Sudhaus that also runs a beer garden. Don't miss the former engine room, unfolding over three floors, which currently hosts themed group exhibitions and solo shows. Kindl's curatorial concept is unusual and exciting, springing from the experienced Swiss hands of Andreas Fiedler. Before you go, make sure to cast a glance into the boiler house, a 20-metre-high, 20-metre-deep, and 20-metre-wide space in which one artist per year is allowed to realise a piece. On the occasion of the space's opening, the artist Roman Signer (born 1938) suspended a yellow Kitfox prop-plane from the ceiling, mounting strong fans on the walls that make it move. A horrifying concept to any phobics out there, he must have been moved by the boiler room's atypical dimensions. Then again, maybe the reasons were a bit more mundane. Maybe he got the idea after enjoying a cool bottle of cherry schnapps; something like that can certainly lead to a quick comedown. Art and alcohol are often inseparable, you can see it in the history of this building.

An Unusual Alternative to the Sofa Bed

What do you think's more stable: your nerves or the springs inside a couch made up as a guest bed? In the end it doesn't matter, for they come all the same – friends, family, friends of family, and the family of friends. Living in Berlin you silently accept the fact that you'll always have to be ready for visitors. I do not doubt that some people put out terrariums with spiders and snakes just to appear less attractive hosts.

Most of the time you're happy to lead people through the city or to do something together. And most of the time you don't mind having to tiptoe past the guest-room or sofa in order to set the table. For those who have neither the desire nor the room to offer

HÜTTENPALAST
HOBRECHTSTRASSE 65 / 66
12047 BERLIN
TEL. 030 373 05 806
OFFICE DAILY 9AM – 6PM, CAFÉ FROM 7AM
WWW.HUETTENPALAST.DE

guests a roof over their heads, there are of course thousands of hotels, hostels, pensions, and Airbnbs in the city. And then there is also the Hüttenpalast, an idea for a hotel that was one of a kind when it started: spread throughout two huge factory halls are six differently decorated, nostalgically oriented campervans and small cabins. Each of these refuges has its own individually decorated area with seats and tables, and every guest has their own private, lockable space to retreat to when they want. The arrangements look like a wonderful photomontage or art project, but everything here has been coordinated to guarantee an unforgettable and unique stay. But who

on earth would come up with such an idea? Fashion designer Sarah and events manager Silke. Both had been happily living in their neighbourhood of Neukölln for quite a while before they realised it was time for a change. They wanted to host people from all over the world and that in a city that was already well used to tourists and prepared to match any of their expectations. As fate would have it, the spaces of a former furniture manufacturer and vacuum-cleaner factory became available. In 2010, the two went to work. They planned, built, designed, and planted. And then they came up with the idea of the campervans. That was it: camping reconsidered with care and comfort. You step into the Hüttenpalast through a cosy café where guests can have breakfast. A door leads to the partially roofed inner courtyard with its flowerpots, climbing plants, seating areas, and bench swings. From here you walk into the two large halls. I would love to have cast a glance into every one of the campervans; everything has been so lovingly taken care of and is so unconventional. I ask Sarah whether guests are ever bothered by the proximity of other guests, whether perhaps young people were their only guests. No, those kinds of apprehensions disappear immediately. People who want to spend the night here know that they're in for something different. Noise? No. Sounds? Of course. But you hear things in other places too. On top of it, people of all ages are very considerate of each other. Once, right at the beginning, a few pensioners ran into a group of young backpackers from the US. Just a little while later they were all sitting together in the courtyard, talking and drinking wine. For people who enjoy singular experiences but would rather sleep in a conventional bed, they also have a few classic-style hotel rooms. You should without a doubt come have a look at this special place – even if you run the risk of immediately falling in love and giving up your friend's couch.

Tastes Great, and Good for Your Karma Too

RESTLOS GLÜCKLICH
DONAUSTRASSE 15
12043 BERLIN
RESERVATIONS:
WWW.RESTLOS-GLUECKLICH.BERLIN

Colour and size were the criteria my grandmother employed when buying eggs. Compulsory labelling, introduced country-wide by law in 2004, didn't exist yet. Labels like 'organic' or 'ethical handling' were not part of the discussion: she bought her eggs right from the butcher, whose spacious courtyard hosted a few happily cackling chickens. And the laying date? To see if an old egg was still fresh enough, she'd put it in a water glass. If it stayed at the bottom, you could eat it; if it came to the top, it went to the compost pile. Mould on the marmalade was scooped out with a spoon, and it wasn't the stamp on the bottle but my Grandma's nose that decided whether milk

was still good. Mouldy bread was only tossed with a sigh. Today, most people just pay attention to the sell-by date, mistakenly equating it with the expiration date. And as a result, yogurts, sauces, and pasta – and, in fact, every eighth item of food we purchase – go straight to the rubbish bin, which is nonsense, as most of those products are still totally fine.

A fact that doesn't allow Annette Keuchel and Leonie Beckmann a moment's rest. They founded the Restlos Glücklich association in order to sensitise people to a more conscious consumption of, and appreciation for, food. With hefty doses of idealism, realism, persuasive power, and stamina, the two developed a way of dealing with the products we consume that won over more and more fans every day. The next logical step for the two was to open the restaurant, Restlos Glücklich, where they would only cook with food that could no longer be sold. Naturally, these ingredients are not spoilt; they even abide by the sell-by date. But many producers and supermarkets remove products from sale when they are bent, bruised, or otherwise damaged. The cooking crew gets their ingredients from partner companies in the mornings, and then at noon the head chef decides what healthy and nutritious meals he will prepare from them. Believe me: qualitatively speaking there is absolutely no difference with going to a regular restaurant. It's just that you'll gain some good karma points, as the concept behind Restlos Glücklich is worthy of support in many ways. The profits allow for six paid positions, everyone else is a volunteer. And don't think this set-up takes away from other charities, the restaurant naturally also works with organisations like the Berliner Tafel food bank. A further element of their work is organising workshops and cooking classes. 'Children can learn to have so much fun working with food', says Keuchel, herself a mother. 'They often have no idea where food comes from or how you prepare it. Once children develop a connection to cooking, they begin to eat more healthily and no longer throw things away so easily.'

And speaking of karma, not too long ago the former pop-up restaurant found a fixed location: a little place that's almost too good to be true, located directly on the Maybachufer in Kreuzberg. If you want to see what they cook up, reserve a place beforehand. You can do so online, and what's more: the chef can calculate how much to cook, so not a single scrap gets thrown out.

Tempelhof, Schöneberg

Flowers, Skaters, and a Lot of Sky

In Berlin, this urban wasteland is something like the proud hippie among the city's other areas. Beloved, sought-after, romanticised, furnished with beehives, and planted by some; considered unattractive and passé by others who throw their hands above their heads and say: 'You've got to be kidding! Empty land! Where on earth are you going to find something like that? Berlin just keeps growing and growing, something just has to be built here, new apartments, for example. There's no other way to handle the numbers of migrants and refugees, or do you want to put them out on the edges of the city?' Well, not in our backyard. During negotiations over what

TEMPELHOFER FELD
12101 BERLIN

is arguably the largest amount of open space in the city, the former runways of Tempelhof airport, arguments, counter-arguments, and various sensitivities were all thrown into a giant mixer called a referendum, the results of which turned out to be a green smoothie for the city's soul. That which was free to remain free; the wasteland won. Naturally, this was preceded by a real back and forth. By now, however, the area's come into its own, for everyone knows how symbolically important it is. During the Berlin Blockade, Tempelhof airport kept the heart of Berlin beating, especially through the Air Lift, when 9,000 tons of foodstuffs and goods were flown into the city daily. This enormous undertaking ended in 1949, and in the following decades there was regular air traffic. In 2008, the airport was closed. But what was the city supposed to do with an area almost as big as 450 football fields right in the middle of the city? Various plans and concepts were discussed, and the city government even floated the idea of 'perimeter development'. 70 of the 300 hectares were supposed to be sliced off for three new developments containing around 4,700 apartments, commercial spaces, and a central as well as regional library. But none of this was to happen, as a referendum was held on the future of the airport in 2014, and 64%

of voters voted against any form of development. And that is now law. Of course, laws can be replaced by new laws, but whether they ever will remains unclear. The Tempelhofer Field is a charismatic and pretty surreal place. Where else will you find such a vista in a city as large as Berlin? Not a single building, not even a tree breaks the horizontal plane trimmed with paths and covered with grass. A small bit of the area is used for urban gardening, with close to 600 hobby gardeners having worked here since 2010. What has emerged is a fascinating, fragrant, colourful, and buzzing patchwork of gardens with benches but without any fences, open to all. In addition to the garden projects, numerous artistic and social projects have emerged on the Tempelhofer Field; all with just a few simple rules and the express desire that you be involved. Having said that, you are also welcome to just lie in the grass and stare up at the sky, take a walk, go jogging, roller-skating, skateboarding, walk your dog, or even go kite surfing. At the Columbiadamm entrance there is a beer garden, otherwise the only things you will find in this immense open space are clouds, kites, flowers, birds, sun, rain, other people, a bit of asphalt, and grass. Where else would you find something like this?

Street Art Goes Museum

URBAN NATION
MUSEUM FOR URBAN CONTEMPORARY ART
BÜLOWSTRASSE 7
10783 BERLIN
TEL. 030 322 95 989
TUE. – SUN. 10AM – 6PM
WWW.URBAN-NATION.COM

When I was a child, though a lot of what we have today wasn't around, but we had other stuff that made up for it: nuns in their habits, for example, were a part of the urban landscape, as were travel agencies and record shops. The inner city was sprinkled with so-called department stores that sold writing paper, bras, pipe tobacco, cats, hot-water bottles, soft-serve ice cream, and joke books. A department store was like a miniature version of the Internet, but full of things you could immediately take home. Back then, troupes of guys with dark moustaches and colourful ponchos would stand in pedestrian zones and play upbeat music, and when they were

done, they would pass a sombrero around to collect money. And in the same way that street musicians belonged to the pedestrian areas, so did artists. Street art was made by people who drew medium-sized pictures on the ground – most of the time takes on the Mona Lisa or Virgin Mary. No one painted on walls (why would they?), or if they did then simply scrawling phrases like FASCIST PIGS OUT and NO NUKES. Maybe the time of slogans is past, you see them ever so rarely these days. But what has come all the more strongly into focus is what is known as urban street art, a kind of art that is just about omnipresent on the streets of Berlin. Everything has become a canvas: facades, underpasses, streetlights, firewalls, bridges – basically anything that doesn't move. These surfaces are painted, sprayed, stickered, and even blown up. The art comes in sizes both big and small, abstract and realistic, but equal in one aspect: all are essentially ephemeral. Sooner or later the images will disappear at the hand of their natural enemies: some due to wind and weather, most to demolition and renovation. The highly talented street-artists from all over the world know this; nevertheless, they spill their talent all over the place with abandon, granting their art a turbulent affair with the city's canvases. In Berlin, there have always been both illegal graffiti and tags as well as skilful legal murals. But since the time Iceland-born Yasha Young first took up urban street art here, the art form's quantity and quality have developed into something quite new. Young – who has run her own galleries in Brooklyn, London, and Berlin and boasts some of the best international contacts in the art scene – made and makes every effort to give the most diverse street artists the possibility of having their work and their ideas appear legally throughout the cityscape of Berlin. She works together with the senate, property owners, and housing associations, who have an interest of their own in seeing their buildings' facades turned into something eye-catching, even if only for a limited time. If you're interested in this kind of art, I strongly encourage you to make your way to Bülowstrasse, where the entryways, facades, and pillars function as a kind of open-air gallery. In cooperation with a dedicated foundation, Young has also succeeded in opening the world's very first street-art museum in that very same neighbourhood in the autumn of 2017. Its motto: 'Connect. Create.

Care.' Together with street artists and through the medium of art, it has initiated and supported international social projects. A few of the projects have been documented and can be seen at the museum, just like a lot of other things waiting to be discovered on-site. Entrance is free. Art really cannot be made any easier.

The City's Best Cocktails

VICTORIA BAR
POTSDAMER STRASSE 102
10785 BERLIN
TEL. 030 257 59 977
SUN. - THU. 6.30PM - 3AM,
FRI. - SAT. 6.30PM - 4AM
WWW.VICTORIABAR.DE

In the mood for a Raspberry Gin Fizz? 'Thanks, Bettina, really, but no.' If you get around as much as my friend does – Tokyo, New York, London – and are familiar with the most exclusive bars and first-rate cocktails, you no longer care to do without a certain level of quality. Sure, my friend also knows how narrow-minded that sounds. There are many cocktail bars in Berlin, of course, but can any hold its own on the international level? Still, I ask him whether he wants to come with me. We've got two hours to kill after all. 'I guess, no problem.'

The Victoria Bar is pleasantly crowded. This evening I take a seat at the bar. My companion takes a look around. 'Nice place',

he says almost begrudgingly. 'I know', I think, 'just wait.'

At its birth in 2001, founders Beate Hindermann and Stefan Weber knew they had brought a lovely bar into the world, one that over the years would become even better and more self-assured without ever falling prey to the capital city's erratic trends. The photos, lights, paintings, furniture, colours: everything has been thought out and stylishly arranged. But no matter how appealing the look, the heart of a bar beats behind the counter, where all the special ingredients, bottles, glasses, and utensils are to be found, where the artists and alchemists work, the ones who matter. Or it does

if your order entails more than *Sekt* on ice – and it should when you're in what's arguably the best cocktail bar in all of Berlin. And should you be or get hungry you can choose from a selection of warm or cold dishes. 'The drinks must be impeccable', says Beate, 'or you have no business allowing yourself to converse casually with your guests.' Discipline, passion, experience, warmth, and a soft spot for Elvis – these five attributes describe Beate pretty well. She is a full-blooded gourmet. She keeps a close eye over her bar with an astonishing, from a medical point of view, 360-degree range. The fact that most of the Victoria team has been there for years, if not from the very beginning, says a lot about her instincts.

I drink a Brandy Alexander, something I copied from the singer Olli Schulz, who completely floored me with his order. Gives you a Faye Dunaway feeling, and it tastes remarkably good. My companion wants to try it, of course. I hear 'top-notch' and see his hand reach for the drinks menu. The end result is the reversal of his hesitation, the reformation of a sceptic, the greeting of a future regular. I know that he will recommend the bar to others. Not that it's necessary, though the *New York Times* did so too. It listed the Victoria Bar as one of its "5 Places to Go in Berlin".

Turkish Specialties Made with Love

MEYAN
GOLTZSTRASSE 36
10781 BERLIN
TEL. 030 754 42 540
MON. - SAT. 10AM - 10PM,
SUN. 10AM - 5PM
WWW.MEYAN-BERLIN.DE

Whenever I used to clear the table after parties or rinse the silverware in between meals, my mother liked to say: 'Bettina worked in the service industry for seven years, you know.' She put particular emphasis on the word service, as if I had discovered the Amber Room or a cure for cancer. I waited tables during grammar school and later on at university, just like many others, all of whom know as well as I do that the gastronomy world is a tough place. Aside from the hours, it is really hard to establish yourself as a new café or restaurant. If you're unlucky, you end up with the wrong customers; if you're unluckier, you don't even get those. Perhaps the com-

petition is too strong, the cook ill too often, the staff too small, the location poor, or maybe you're lacking in experience, money, or, quite simply, joy. All of these breaking points contribute to the fact that close to 70% of new restaurants close their doors within just two years.

Imagine a young German couple of Turkish descent wanting to establish their own concept in a street crammed full of other cafés and restaurants. Key data: two small children, little time, limited budget, a worn space, and no gastronomical experience at all. Are the chances of making it really 50:50, as Cigdem, one of the founders in question, tells me? I think this 50:50 split ap-

plies quite well to Cigdem herself, who will, depending on the circumstances, either cheerfully interject that the strategy had to do with 'our Turkish blood' or, just a little while later, that some things no doubt had to do with the fact that she's from southern Germany, 'a Schwabian by birth.' In retrospect, it was a downright gift that neither the qualified fashion designer nor her husband Ani, who works as an actor and moderator, had really envisioned all the risks beforehand. They forged ahead without thinking twice, knocked down old walls, scoured analogue and digital flea markets to find the appropriate furnishings, refurbished the furniture, painted the walls in warm colours, and combined their love of old things with a lot of the new. In 2013, the rather roomy and very comfortable modern Turkish restaurant/café Meyan was the result. It is located on Goltzstrasse, which, if no longer a real artery, is still a strong vein running through Schöneberg. The centrepiece is a large glass display case filled with countless delicacies you can pick and choose from. On the menu you'll find modern and traditional Turkish specialties like *fırında tavuk, tavuklu kuşkonmaz, gırık*, or *karnıyarık*. There is a large selection of breakfast items, and you can even purchase homemade marmalades, soap made from donkeys and goats' milk, towels and handbags, and colourful dishes and bowls. And books. In 2011, Cigdem's sisters founded the Berlin-based binooki-Verlag, which publishes, among other things, novels, crime fiction, children's books, and modern classics by Turkish authors in German translation. Naturally, there are also cookbooks.

To sum up: the place is hopping. These two culinary novices have done everything right. Their secret? Quality. Friendliness. The fact that they do everything with love. And that they work like mad.

18

U4 VIKTORIA-LUISE-PLATZ

A Charming Austrian Restaurant

SISSI
MOTZSTRASSE 34
10777 BERLIN
TEL. 030 210 18 17
DAILY FROM 5PM
WWW.SISSI-BERLIN.DE

My friend Miranda rents out *fincas* on Mallorca. She is a born host: professional, friendly, creative. The holiday guests are almost always really happy. Then come the follow-ups: the reviews. 'Hey, what a holiday, everything was great, but one day all of a sudden a flock of sheep wearing bells walked past the house – all that ringing for two hours and the following day our kid stepped in sheep shit. 3 out of 5 stars.' Or someone who found everything magnificent. Everything, that is, except the glasses, which were plentiful, by the way. But seeing as that his family consists of six people, he was annoyed by the fact that he couldn't always have six iden-

tical glasses on the table. 3.5 out of 5 stars.

Ratings are a basic democratic decision-making tool you have to use responsibly, especially considering those on the receiving end often depend on them for their professional existence. We all must be sure to act carefully and responsibly. For sooner or later this whole circus of ratings and sensitivities could lead to no one risking anything new at all. My most negative experience with this whole issue took place during a warm summer evening I spent at Sissi with some friends. I had taken them there because it is an extremely charming and, as far as Berlin is concerned, atypically intimate restaurant that serves Austrian food and the world's best dessert. 'It doesn't matter what you order, *Backhendl*, *Saftgulasch*, or *Wiener Schnitzel*, or even if you're a vegetarian – order whatever you want, you'll be happy. But promise me one thing: for dessert we're all going to have the apricot dumplings.' Agreed. The apricot dumplings with nut butter and raspberry foam are, and I'm not exaggerating, the best dessert I have ever eaten, by a long shot.

Head chef and owner Martin Hartmann, Austrian and proud descendant of a traditional baker, completed his chef's training at the Hospizhotel am Arlberg, a 5-star hotel. After stints running his own restaurants in France, Switzerland, and Salzburg, Martin opened Sissi on Motzstrasse in 2007. There I was, sitting with five friends of mine, me, the dessert godmother, eager to order six portions of apricot dumplings. But Martin regretfully shook his head and shrugged. 'What do you mean? Aren't there any left?' 'No, we took them off the menu.' It felt like a wrecking ball had just smashed against my head. 'Very funny.' 'No, really, we got such a bad review, a woman didn't like the dumplings, no idea, maybe something was a bit different that evening, but, as a restaurant, you just can't risk something like that any more.' I was really angry at that unknown woman. And I was in pain. Seeing as I was not the only apricot-dumpling junkie – countless other guests also registered their despair over the loss – they are now back on the menu. For me they are the most important reason to eat here regularly, though certainly not the only one. In addition to the dumplings, the prices are fair; the meat comes from properly kept animals; the Schilcher rosé, a sparkling one, tastes like it has bathed in currants; and the delicious homemade bread can even be bought to take home. The two downstairs rooms are not particularly large. They're cosy, especially in winter, when the pot-bellied wood-burning stove radiates warmth from its stomach. In summer, most guests choose to sit outside. And if it's too full or you've got a large party, you can go up to the first floor, where there is room for up to 60 people. Those yet unfamiliar with Austrian German can familiarise themselves with the not insignificant differences from Germany's German. If you're in the mood for crêpes and you order *Palatschinke*, make sure to stress the I and leave off the N at the end. Though it may sound like it has birds or *Vögel* in it, vegetarians should feel at ease ordering the *Vogerlsalat*, as it's just the Austrians' version of lamb's lettuce. Sissi's staff are happy to relieve any doubts and will happily and effortlessly guide all non-Austrians through the menu.

19

U1 / U2 / U3 / U4 NOLLENDORFPLATZ

Wunderkammer Full of Finds

ANTIQUARIAT THOMAS MERTENS
WINTERFELDTSTRASSE 51
10781 BERLIN
TEL. 030 251 9203
MON. - SAT. 11AM - 6PM

I saw a three-headed mink trying to escape from an ostrich egg. I saw green-glowing scarabs, as big as my palm, trapped under glass. And a number of spiky pufferfish dangling from the ceiling on wires, right next to a pair of stuffed birds with glassy eyes, there, beside an ancient circus poster.

This is no dream, no drugged-out hallucination, no scene from an experimental film, simply the kinds of things you run into at Thomas Mertens' highly unusual antiques shop. His store is a cabinet of wonders, like a fantastical place packed with fantastical creatures, images, and books that have nothing to do with the present time or everyday reality.

You won't find this kind of selection at any flea market, not even the most exclusive ones. These are sought-after one-of-a-kinds from a mysterious past, picked up here and there. Walking into the shop, your mental muscles start flexing as your imagination is immediately triggered. Who collected all these iridescent insects? Were they hanging above the worn-out sofa of a seedy scientist, bent over his illegible notes deep into the night? What ocean did these strange fish swim through? With all those spikes, how do they even reproduce? Are they born that way or is this some kind of jackalope creation? Are there really forests somewhere in the world

where you can find butterflies like these flying through the air? How nice not to immediately have an answer to everything. Standing inside or out in front of the shop window you just marvel in silence before realising how seldom you actually do this: simply marvel.

Thomas Mertens has a lot of experience and a good hand for all kinds of finds. During the first years of his business, the professional art historian concentrated on antiquarian books, which he actually still sells. Online platforms, however, made this market rather volatile, so Mertens decided to expand his selection. In addition to posters, cards, paintings, books, and various bizarre objects, he now also sells contemporary photography. I ask him if there are any objects in his shop that he wouldn't sell. He could separate himself from all of it, he says. Fair enough, but surely there's something he has been quietly waiting to come across all these years, a longed-for chance find, an undiscovered bookmark in an old book, a yellowed postcard with a blue Mauritius stamp? Mertens briefly laughs. No, he's not waiting for anything in particular. Recently though, someone brought him two hand-written pages on the effects of wine dating from the

8th century. Then his heart indeed skipped a beat.

My heart, for what it's worth, skips a beat every time I catch a glimpse of the 40 million-year-old dinosaur teeth, which cost 90 euros a piece. 'Mr Mertens', I say, 'I can't even think back 500,000 years, let alone 40 million years. For only 90 euros? That comes to just 0,00000225 cents a year! Something's not quite right here.' Mr Mertens remains calm. 'The whole Moroccan desert is full of them. It was a sea once, and the sand has conserved the teeth pretty well. The ones I have here belonged to the smaller ones, the saurians.' Forty million years? 20,000 years ago, Berlin was still covered by a giant Scandinavian ice sheet. Fascinated, my brains still smouldering slightly, I leave. By the time I walk past again the next morning and look into the window, everything will be healed and ready to be set aflame anew.

God's Green Thumb is Called Mike

CHURCH GARDEN OF ST MATTHIAS
WINTERFELDTPLATZ
10781 BERLIN

It all began nine years ago. Small changes morphed into big ones, and then from one day to the next it was impossible to ignore. All of a sudden, the green space in front of the St-Matthias church looked like someone had covered the house of worship in lush photographic wallpaper. There, where for years only unhappy bushes and city-dust-covered ivy had proliferated, flowers were growing, blossoms were bursting off of branches, bees and bumblebees were buzzing, and butterflies were fluttering about in their brightly coloured Versace garb. What happened? In Berlin you immediately think someone must be shooting a movie. Wrong. Someone had begun to plant the garden spaces in front of, behind, and alongside the church; it was a wild tangle, yet it had a certain system. Hollyhocks, roses, sunflowers, larkspur, lupines. Amazed, people stopped in their tracks, took photos, or carefully began to smell the blooms. 'Long live the church tax', I thought. Until one crepuscular evening, at least, when coming home late from work I spied a bearded man in the middle of one of the plots. Plucking here and pulling there, running the sweat-covered back of his hand across his forehead to wipe away a strand of hair, he then picked up more dirt. This wasn't a flower-thief, but God's own green thumb, the man who's got everything under control here.

Mike lives in the immediate vicinity of the church, he studied gardening and landscaping and works in a men's clothing store. 'One day I was walking along here when I saw a bride and groom having themselves photographed out in front of the church – with two-metre high nettles in the background! I immediately thought of my grandfather, who would have thrown his hands over his head. "That just won't do: you've got to stand in front of roses."' Mike applied to become the guardian of the garden, which no one was taking care of and which formally belongs to the city – and he got started right away. Every free minute he could spare he spent getting rid of cigarette butts, dog faeces, used needles, rubbish, and fast-food wrappers. He loosened up the dirt, fertilised and watered it, planted and seeded. Did the city at least help him out a bit financially? Mike shakes his head. Well, was the church a bit more generous, seeing as that he had created a Garden of Eden right in front of their doors? Well, two years ago they spent money on a water connection after seeing an article about Mike in the paper. Before that, he had to haul every litre of water with a watering can from the square out front, but Mike only explains that if you ask directly. He'd rather talk about positive things; people do enough complaining.

He pays for the plants out of his own pocket. Now and again people in the neighbourhood give him some money. On good days, people come to the store where he works and leave a donation so that he can buy new flowers because, sadly, they get stolen over and over again. The nerve! Right from the front yard of the almighty, who in response to my request for an interview only stated he was on holiday, but that

he'd already said what he had to say: 'You will reap what you sow' (known to the yoga generation as karma). Once, a homeless person pressed the € 2 he'd made over the previous hour into Mike's hand. 'With it he said: "I'm grateful to you. I'm sharing my money with you because you're taking care of this garden." I accepted it because I wanted to respect his gesture.'

Mike isn't Catholic, but that's unimportant. 'I think you can also find God in nature. This garden is the place where I speak with him.'

Prayers embedded in the flowerbeds. 'Exactly, that's what I believe.' Mike is the friendly, reserved type. He retains this friendliness even when talking about all the bureaucratic hoops that accompany the church garden. His request was pushed through countless offices; it took six whole years for it to be approved. His voice, however, does go up a notch when he says that he had to pledge to restore the biotope to its former condition the day he was ready to give up. Back to wasteland, garbage, abandonment. It's absurd. Personal initiatives should not be hampered but rewarded. 'Ach, well, I'm going to keep on going as long as I can, health-wise and money-wise, as long as it continues to make people happy.' Mike for mayor.

Brazil Meets Berlin

ATELIER CULINÁRIO
SABINE HECK
KYFFHÄUSERSTRASSE 21
10781 BERLIN
RESERVATIONS AND BOOKINGS THROUGH
WWW.SABINEHUECK.DE

Everything was better in Germany, on that much both of her grandmothers in Brazil agreed. There weren't any long queues in front of the banks, the streets were well paved, and the cherries and strawberries tasted sublime. 'Your mouth would just explode with happiness, little Sabine', they'd say. Sabine's two grandmothers originally came from Berlin, migrating to South America at different times and for different reasons. Because their old homeland could not say anything in response, it became idealised in their absence. Which is what often happens: places get idealised into objects of longing, one that in this case ended up actually meeting the expectations of

to Berlin. Today, Sabine Hueck runs the little Atelier Culinário in Schöneberg, a sometimes restaurant and now-and-again café. The Atelier is like a treasure chest: a kitchen studio, an event location, and a secret place. Here, all the threads of her life come together.

A few years ago, she began to write books. Wonderful cookbooks full of recipes in which she, like a proud father of the bride, gently leads the traditional to the new in order to allow something special to grow out of it. She completed a book for the Foreign Office on German cuisine, but naturally it also discusses her Brazilian background. And typical Brazilian cuisine? She wouldn't know. 'The most typical thing about it is that all the cultures there are mixed: Italians, Japanese, Portuguese, indigenous people, Africans, Germans. It's the perfect combination, that's what I'd call Brazilian cuisine.'

Describing this woman is not without its risks. Words like natural come to mind, friendly, radiant, open-minded. In her atelier she introduces people to cooking, works on recipes, hosts parties, shoots instructional videos, and has trouble giving her opening times and programme (cooking courses, pop-up dinners, etc.)

the young girl born and raised in São Paolo. Sabine was 12 the first time she came to Germany, and 18 when she decided to stay. To her parents' horror, she nurtured the desire to dedicate her life to the culinary arts, to cooking and baking, and to the joy of innumerable friends, guests, and customers. It's a desire she has never abandoned. And how she got started? A Hospitality Management programme in Munich, a job at the Four Seasons, a foray into the world of Waldorf education. She became a mother when still rather young, went back to Brazil, founded a bakery 'with cake recipes from here and exotic fruits from Brazil, that went great', then she returned any kind of regularity. What's typically German about this is probably missing precisely that sense of order. And leaving it all open typically Brazilian. Sometimes that's just the way it goes, and sometimes, with all her projects and plans, Sabine Hueck runs up against what is feasible in terms of time. That is no doubt the primary reason why her atelier is not open every day. If you're interested in diving into this little refugium, this kitchen space with its GDR-era garden chairs and tables from bars in Leipzig, its lights, candles, colours, and flowers, you'll have to do a little bit of research on her website beforehand. Have a look to see if there's still a space on her cooking class, led by Sabine herself or one of her top-class chef friends from around the world. Or go to one of the rare dinners, hosted, for example, by 2-star chef Michael Kempf. Just a few days later there's a 'collective cooking class with Kaoru Iriyama', who studied with one of the most important of Japanese chefs. End up in Atelier Culinário once and you will be sure to return. Sabine knows that. And if she happens to forget, she can have a look online. Hardly anything can top a guest writing that they felt like they had 'eaten love'.

For Farewells, Arrivals, And Quiet Moments

CEMETERY CAFÉ FINOVO
ENTRANCE THROUGH THE STONE
JUGENDSTIL GATE
ALTER ST.-MATTHÄUS-KIRCHHOF
GROSSGÖRSCHENSTRASSE 12-14
10829 BERLIN
TEL. 030 206 15 520
WED. - SUN. 10AM - 8PM,
TUE. 12PM - 8PM
RUN BY BERND BOSSMANN
(AKA ICHGOLA ANDROGYN)
WWW.CAFE-FINOVO.DE

CEMETERY OF THE ZWÖLF-APOSTEL-
KIRCHENGEMEINDE
KOLONNENSTRASSE 24-25

My father died when I was six. Whenever I accompanied my mother to the cemetery, I'd feel ashamed at my impulse to want to take the flowers from all the other graves home, my thinking that they'd just go to rot there in any case. I was never overcome by the expected or appropriate sadness. On the contrary, I was happy whenever it was finally time to go; at the graveyard you had to be quiet, and everywhere you looked old women with serious faces were whispering to one another and weeding.

Sometimes, there'd be a few young people sitting around on the ground in front of the headstone next to my father's. I liked that better. They rolled ciga-

rettes, spoke loudly, and gesticulated wildly. The name BENNO OHNESORG was chiselled into the stone. 'He was a left-wing activist', my mother said tersely, as if a young child would have any idea what that meant.

When I was around 16, I visited Paris' Père Lachaise cemetery with my friend Kuno. 'A god is buried here, Bettina', he said in a serious voice, 'Jim Morrison of the Doors'. there must have been at least 70 people around his grave, smoking joints and listening to music.

As for me, I have never felt any particular connection to cemeteries, not enough to make me want to commemorate a particular person there. Having said that, I have since gotten to know one of these places, and it has given me a hint of just how incomparable the atmosphere of places like this can be. I discovered it by chance. A few years ago, I brought my car in to be repaired and had to wait two hours. I decided to find out what the old wall next to the repair shop was all about. It stretched all the way down to the next intersection and then disappeared behind some buildings. I walked halfway down the block and suddenly found myself standing in front of the stone gate of the St.-Matthäus cemetery. And

I certainly would not have ventured inside had I not noticed the quaint-looking café right at the entrance. There were a lot of different kinds of flowerpots, a bunch of tables and chairs thrown together, some little figurines, odds and ends. All very informal and familiar. The cake was wonderful ('Homemade!'), and a guest at the next table explained to me that this was a rather special cemetery. 'It's located in a special place, and it's especially queer.' Aside from soldiers and former parishioners, there were a lot of important people like the physician Rudolf Virchow and the Brothers Grimm. And numerous gravestones bear the names of people who fought for the rights and acceptance of bisexuals and homosexuals in different ways throughout their lives. The singer Rio Reiser is among them, the filmmaker Manfred Salzgeber, the painter Gustav Richter, and the drag legend and political activist Ovo Maltine. A local association (EFEU) organises the care and sponsorship of the culturally and historically important graves, and once a year offers an educational tour entitled 'Kreuz & Queer' (a play on the expression 'kreuz und quer', which means 'this way and that'). In addition, they offer various events in the aforementioned Café Finovo, a name that is composed of the words for 'end' (*fin*) and 'new beginning' (*novo*).

One of the cemetery's pathways is bisected by the S-Bahn, which every few minutes rumbles along the railway line like a colourful caterpillar. From the other side, you can sometimes hear the sound of children's cries – of course, there's a nursery there. And that's exactly the point: Finovo. This is how a place for farewells should sound: not full of reprimands, but with space for the everyday sounds of those who are still here, those who mourn their dead and continue to live.

Dahlem, Wannsee, Zehlendorf

Wood & Vesper

GRUNEWALD LAKE
14193

CHALET SUISSE
IM JAGEN 5 / CLAYALLEE 99
14195 BERLIN
TEL. 030 832 6362
DAILY 12PM - 10PM
WWW.CHALET-SUISSE.DE

Compared to other cities, Berlin is still that wild thing with the smudged eyeliner, runs in its hose, and the stubborn desire to drink everybody else under the table. There are copious places in this city that could be considered decadent and disreputable – depending on the criteria you choose to apply. And I don't mean those establishments with a sign saying ROSIE'S GARDEN OF LUST over the door. With the greatest matter-of-factness, clubs like Berghain or Wilde Renate throw sex parties for people who don't live in Sodom or Gomorrah, but in Charlottenburg or Friedrichshain, and who during the day work at the organic market or go to university. This

erotic trend has established itself in the capital, but it really isn't all that new.

In 1891, for example, the refined Grunewald hunting lodge played host to a legendary orgy including many aristocrats, among them fifteen well-known members of the imperial court. After a number of historical letters surfaced, some rather risqué details came to light, ones I cannot risk going into here. But you can have a look for yourself if you take a walk around Grunewald Lake. The area can be reached from various sides, and the hike is fascinating whatever the season; it's a great favourite among dog owners, as it is one of the few areas in the city that doesn't have a leash law (this may have been different at historical bondage parties). And yes, you will indeed pass the aforementioned little Renaissance-style castle. Built in 1542, it is considered the oldest in Berlin. In the lodge's café you can enjoy a piece of cake, have a coffee, and wonder how you managed not to stumble over the bumpy cobblestones which grace the courtyard.

On autumn or winter days I recommend you walk just a little bit further through the Grunewald, straight to Chalet Suisse, which, so far at least, has not been associated with any licentious behaviour.

Founded by the personal chef of Federal President Lübke, this typical Swiss tavern nestled in the middle of the woods boasts a large beer garden and a playground. Considering its name, no one will be surprised to learn that the key culinary focus is on Swiss cuisine. Naturally, the Helvetian head chef is a master of various *Rösti* (hash browns) specialities, and he knows just how Zurich-style veal strips should taste. The salmon is their house specialty, cooked on the restaurant's own wood-fired grill. Those in the know order an Allgäuer beer or, depending on the time of year, a glass of cider. All the products are organic, and they serve quality meat from Neuland.

Also ask about their many cheese specialties. When the wood in the fireplace crackles and you're tackling a hefty portion of Raclette or fondue, a day that seemed a bit iffy at first can turn into a real gift from heaven.

This Trip is Totally Organic

BOTANICAL GARDEN AND MUSEUM
KÖNIGIN-LUISE-STRASSE 6-8
14195 BERLIN
TEL. 030 838 50 100
DAILY 9AM - 7/8PM
OPENING HOURS CAN BE FOUND AT
WWW.BGBM.ORG

My first real boyfriend was a bit odd. Sometimes he seemed to have a screw loose. At those moments he and his mate would engage in existential posturing and read, smoke, and debate for days and nights on end, making a big show of running their hands through their hair whenever they caught sight of their reflection in the windowpanes. They felt like they were French existentialists, and as soon as the opportunity arose, they began to experiment with psychoactive substances. One night, the two of them climbed over the wall of the Botanical Garden and got their hands on some datura plants. This poisonous nightshade is known to have powerful

hallucinogenic effects, though it's hard to get the dosage right. If you don't keel over dead, you can still end up having a bad trip in the worst of cases. And this is exactly what happened to the guys. My boyfriend's friend walked home, left some faecal matter on the front-door mat, grabbed a knife, and kept the family dog in his clutches for a few hours until the effects gradually began to wear off, he slumped over, and slept all the way through to the following day.

Having said that, I imagine that 99.9% of all visitors to the Berlin's Botanical Garden come with noble and quite harmless intentions. We don't have to say all that much about the summer months: everything blooms in a thousand colours, the air buzzes and flutters and smells lovely, and you secretly want to pitch a camouflaged tent so that you can wake up here just once. If you're clever, you'll show up promptly at 9am and only leave when they throw you out at closing time. But it's worth taking a trip in autumn or in winter too. 'Not everything is always in bloom, but something is always blooming', their website says. For example, the Eranthis hyemalis

(*hyemalis* means winter-flowering), the Christmas rose, mistletoe, or the little Amur Adonis rose, which is always teased by the other plants thanks to its macho name. The marsh Labrador tea is also quite familiar with being taunted, but as it is so attractive (and sadly endangered too) everything just rolls off its metaphorical back. As does the snow, for the clever plant has evergreen leaves that hang towards the ground. A good idea. Indeed, you can learn and discover a whole lot of things here. Among the many different gardens, one is scented and another is tactile. There are guided tours, events (tropical nights with cocktails and live music, for example), and – in addition to all the other conservatories – a fascinating tropical house, where even nihilists or atheists must temporarily suspend their stern convictions. Furthermore, they have cacti here that you won't see in any Berlin stairwell or in any old Sunday-afternoon Western. Incidentally, the biggest cactus-thorns used to be used as gramophone needles. That time's gone. Today you could carefully nail them into the wall and hang a bag of USB-sticks off of them.

Art, Coffee, and Culture

MUTTER FOURAGE AM WANNSEE
GALERIE MUTTER FOURAGE
CHAUSSEESTRASSE 15
14109 BERLIN
TEL. 030 805 2311
SEASONAL OPENING HOURS
OPEN WEEKENDS YEAR-ROUND
WWW.MUTTER-FOURAGE.DE

My aunt has a fireplace she never uses ('it's too dirty'); Lucia usually ties her long, glowing hair into a bun ('gets on my nerves otherwise'); Miranda lives in Mallorca but hasn't gone to the sea in years ('no time'). But that's just how it is: we often don't appreciate the things we have that others envy. 'You've got it good', a friend who was visiting me in Berlin once said. 'You've got the Wannsee lake right there. You must go often, right?' He was wrong. But then I immediately began to think about it. I only need around 25 minutes to get there, and every time I see the water shining through the trees, how painterly the small and large boats look moored to shore

or gliding across the water; it really does feel like a holiday. After a long walk, we sat down on one of the jetties, dipped our feet into the clear water, ate an ice cream, and purred like two happy cats. That was the day I discovered Mutter Fourage, a bit away from the lake. A pavement sign invited people into the courtyard of a small old house.

The path led past a number of flowerpots, the air smelled of lavender and camomile, and it buzzed with bumblebees.

In the front part of the courtyard, they sell plants and herbs. The courtyard itself is encircled by former stables, little buildings, and a barn. From 1863 onwards, the area served the capital's rich and powerful as a place to take the fresh summer air. In the village, which back then was known as Stolpe, this little by little made way for the Colonie Alsen, an ideal upper-class town with both a water and an electricity works, shops, and multiple guesthouses for the vacationers. The man who was bequeathed all this history at birth is named Wolfgang Immenhausen. Here, his descendants founded a flour, forage, and potato operation in 1900. Back then, the buildings were still used to house horses and to store grain and flour; the barn was a coach house; and there was a counting house as well as a residential house. Immenhausen, an actor, gallerist, and publisher, belongs to the few third-genera-tion Wannsee-ers. Together with some friends, he stopped the old farm from being repurposed or even demolished in 1978. He had to come up with a new concept, and he focused on sustainabili-ty and culture. They wanted to live here, to connect with the old but create something new. They were successful. The first thing they founded was a natural food store where 'good organic things were sold. Back then there was hardly any of that, in fact, none at all. And we still don't use any pesticides', Immenhausen says. The trade in plants came later, as did the charming gallery with changing exhibitions, the barn used for concerts, readings, and theatre performances, and last but not least the café with home-made cake and food. Have a seat, relax. Maybe you'll begin to won-der how you could come up with enough money to build a small cottage with a fireplace here on the banks of the lake. But please, if you ever do, make sure you use it.

Charlottenburg, Wilmersdorf

A Public Canteen Above the City's Rooftops

SKYLINE CANTEEN AT THE TELEFUNKEN
BUILDING
ERNST-REUTER-PLATZ 7
10587 BERLIN
TEL. 030 939 397 780
MON. - FRI. 7.30AM - 4PM
DURING ACADEMIC HOLIDAYS
7.30AM - 3PM

Verklempt. Sadly the word was hanging so far back in my wardrobe I'd almost forgotten it. It can be produced by a declaration of love or a eulogy. Music. A glimpse of the mountains, a fire, or the sea. Sometimes it's the wide expanse, sometimes the view. Looking down from a mountain onto the panorama below at best makes you humbly and happily aware of the scale of your existence as it is, so gently – but so impressively – countered by reality. In the words of Reinhard Mey, what seemed so big and so important is suddenly nought and small.

Suffice it to say, I hardly ever find myself up on a mountain. I've never been on top of a light-

house or an oil rig, and I like to live on one of the lower floors of a building, never in an attic. Being close to the ground is more comfortable for me than the view from on high. Going up to the 20th floor of the Telefunken high-rise a few years ago with a film crew, I naturally expected an incredible view, Berlin from the sky. I was doing an interview in the Technical University's cafeteria, which is fittingly called Skyline and not only open to students but the general public too. I walked over to the windows and saw my city stretching off to the horizon. I was immediately captivated. In the movies, being in shock is illustrated by the background going out of fo-

cus or entirely disappearing. And that is exactly how I remember that moment: I felt shocked, intoxicated. The day was sunny, the sky cloudless, the colours brilliant, and the view almost endless in all directions. Directly below me, the large Ernst-Reuter Platz – a roundabout with five exits, one of the city's central distribution hubs – was just a small circle that could have drawn by a finger in the sand. From the ground, all the rooftops, cranes, and spires often seem incongruent, all those various architectural styles, but up here they seemed to live together in friendly coexistence. A guest, one of the employees of the student union told me, had once described the view from up here as an 'architectural goulash'. The Prince of Denmark even visited once. *Fantastik udsigt*, fantastic view, he must have thought. Perhaps he ate some *Schupfnudeln* (potato noodles) or *Spätzle* (egg noodles), or maybe some gnocchi or *Maultaschen* (Swabian ravioli). Carbs are a hit here, and the daily dishes – prepared freshly every day in the rather small kitchen – are straightforward: there's a vegetarian soup, one vegetarian and one meat main, salads, dessert, and, naturally, coffee. It is, after all, a canteen. But in the end it doesn't matter what you eat here: it's wonderful to be so close to the sky. And if you ever feel at odds with Berlin – this is the place to come and quickly reconcile with the hustle and bustle down below.

S-/U-BAHNHOF ZOOLOGISCHER GARTEN

Small Jazz Club Bursting with Mighty Jam Sessions

THE HAT BAR
LOTTE-LENYA-BOGEN 550
10623 BERLIN
DAILY 8PM – 2AM
WWW.THEHATBAR.DE

Back at the beginning of the 1990s, I spent six weeks in San Francisco. I found myself having to quickly brush up my English, because I had received the OK for a TV interview with Jon Bon Jovi. I really couldn't make a fool of myself, so I quickly signed up for a language course. There I was, three hours of class a day and for the first time in my life I didn't know a soul. I walked through the neighbourhood, took street-cars, read the event listings, worked hard, and made a real effort – all to no avail. In all the cafés, restaurants, movie thea-tres, markets, and bars it was like I was wearing an invisibility cloak. No one would get into any kind of longer conversation with

me, nothing. One time I bumped into someone on purpose only to see if I really *had* become invisible. My English got better, my mood worse, and so one night I sat myself down in the small jazz club near my hotel, firmly set on moving my return flight up to the next morning. At the bar I suddenly ending up chatting with a woman, at first a bit hesitantly, then at great speed. It was interesting and fun, she introduced me to her friends, and at long last the ice was broken. As a frenetic and almost unceasing round of applause erupted, it became clear to me that I had completely missed the music. Later I learned that it had been the secret gig of a world-class jazz mu-

sician. Quite frustrating. I made up my mind to spend my remaining evenings in San Francisco at this jazz club and as a result got to know, almost at the finish line, a number of great people whom I really would've liked to spend my first few weeks with. Jazz clubs with live music are curious habitats where you can meet a great variety of people. In these places it's always two in the morning, even at 8pm. The windows are closed or even walled up, decent lighting emphasizes the bar and stage, ice cubes glisten, heads nod to the rhythm, eyes close, hands play invisible bass strings; they just have to move, clap, snap their fingers, or delicately play an air-snare.

Lucky Berlin, city of many jazz clubs. You can't go wrong with a visit to the big guys (A-Trane, B-Flat, Quasimodo, Zigzag Club, Yorkschlösschen), but there are, of course, other pearls, smaller, though no less ambitious. My current favourite is The Hat, located under an S-Bahn overpass: it's long, narrow, and not particularly big. This place does not care to decide, nor does it have to, whether it wants to be a well-stocked bar with nightly live music or a jazz club with first-class cocktails. Night after night, the jam sessions draw local and international musicians, some of them well-known, some on the way there. The environment is exactly what you expect from a great jazz bar: there's no cover charge, and the bartenders are friendly and very professional.

The jam-session stage is no bigger than three upright-bass cases laid end to end. According to a 2010 study, 86% of all jazz musicians smoke. And when the music gets started after 10pm, you can smoke here too, but it's compensated by a good ventilation system.

A Green-Blue Refuge Within the City

Life is more fun with a dog. And it doesn't matter whether your dog's relaxed or snappy, big or small – if you love your animal and have trained it more or less well, you can even have a wonderful time in a big city like Berlin. Dog owners say things like 'Look how cute he is!' and 'This dog is terribly clever.' Dog owners are often blind and, as a rule, unconditional love will stand any test. Or almost any.

Because when no one's watching and Woofy, Fido, or Rocky starts rolling in the remains of some dead animal, this deep affection is put to a tough test. In ten long years, my dog Elli has only done so three times. I can live with this statistic, so I quite innocent-

LIETZENSEE LAKE
WUNDTSTRASSE 40
14057 BERLIN

ly go about my way through the wide wide world. For example, along Lietzensee Lake, a refuge right in the middle of the city intersected by the heavily trafficked Kantstrasse. From nearby, the soft hum of the Autobahn is like a muffled hair dryer in the next room, and really everything in this Charlottenburg neighbourhood is full of buildings and streets. But then, in the centre of it all, suddenly a more than six-hectare-large space appears, one covered by water, melancholic weeping willows, and a little park.

You're never the only walker here, but that's OK. It's nice to share this place with others, to sit down on a grassy space or in one of the adjacent cafés, and look out onto the quiet emerald-green water.

It was one of those sunny Walt-Disney days in the middle of summer, I was ambling along the waterside, taking photos of a dozing heron while butterflies fluttered through the warm air like multi-coloured paper napkins. I would have liked to stay longer but I had to leave in order to record a programme. I walked to my car and called my dog. From a distance of ten me-

tres a biting stench drifted towards me. At seven metres, my face contorted. At five, my upper body bent over reflexively and, shutting my eyes, I only just barely managed to suppress my gag reflex. My dog had rolled around in a long-dead carp that had been spit out of the waters of the Lietzensee. She gave off a brutal stink. I took my shirt out of my bag, tied it tightly around my nose and mouth, lifted the dog up onto the back seat with the ends of my fingers, tied her to the door handle with a tow rope, rolled all the windows down as far as they would go, and, nearly masked, drove all the way to work a strong draft blowing through my car. I cried a little, tears of desperation mixed with colossal disgust. Yes, you love your dog unconditionally, but in some moments you really don't.

Once at the radio station I sought out a bathroom in the basement, put the poor stinking dog into a sink, and, under running water, massaged a half-litre of pink soap into its fur so that the worst traces of dead carp would disappear down the drain in a stream of pink foam.

Probably the Best Coffee in Town

GIRO COFFEE BAR
KNESEBECKSTRASSE 5
10623 BERLIN
TEL. 030 679 68 474
MON. - FRI. 8AM - 7PM, SAT. 9AM - 6PM
WWW.GIROCOFFEEBAR.DE

A bright summer day. In front of the Giro Coffee Bar, almost all the seats were taken.

I found the last free chair and sat down at the table of a very attractive couple. The two didn't speak to each other much, in fact they did not exchange a single word, they seemed immersed in their newspapers. After a few minutes, the woman spoke to me. She asked if I could remember having met her at the Sat1 TV studio. 'Oh dear', I said, 'I'm sorry...' 'I'm Jana.' 'Of course!' I said and reached out my hand to introduce myself to her partner as well. 'I'm Betty.' 'Hi', he responded, 'my name's Moritz.' Then Moritz shook Jana's hand. Aha, the two didn't know each

other at all! The three of us began to talk about this and that. Jana asked Moritz what he did. Well, he had just written a book that would soon be published, and I thought: why don't I invite this friendly and eloquent bloke onto my show, it'd expose him to a few more people. Young authors need the exposure. He liked the idea, but he didn't have a lot of time just then. I asked for his number and promised to have my editor invite him. Once back at home, I put his name into a search engine. Oh man, it was Moritz Rinke, one of the most successful authors and playwrights in the country. He came on the show anyway.

Essentially, this long intro is only to prove that I remember almost every visit to Café Giro. It has to do with the atmosphere, the coffee, and the mix of guests, which clearly is due to the two owners, Ralf Weber, an ad-film producer, and Igor Paasch, the owner. Igor/Giro? Exactly, the anagram is no coincidence. The man not only plays with letters, but with videos, colours, and canvases too. Igor, a native Charlottenburger and artist, is a sharp observer with a lively spirit. He is quick, critical, and humorous, all of which are also reflected in his work. For a while, he studied in London, where Soho's Bar Italia became his living room. There he learned that he was comfortable in this type of public place, 'the relaxed feeling invited a certain kind of casualness'.

Well, Berlin is no London and Charlottenburg is no Soho, but in 2011, when the longing for just such a place wouldn't let up even all those years later, he decided to create the place himself. Together with his friend Ralf, he transformed what was, for Berlin standards, a somewhat small space into a familiar coffee bar where students from the Technical University and the University of the Arts could hang out together with academics, people from the neighbourhood, flaneurs, and even the cleaning staff from the hotel next door.

Some of Igor's works hang on the walls. And if your stomach starts to growl, it will be happy to learn that the excellent coffee can be accompanied by sandwiches and soups, crisp croissants, and *pastéis de nata*, all made with love. Did I already mention that striking up a conversation with people there can be rewarding?

A Beautiful Villa Passionate About the Written Word

LITERATURHAUS BERLIN
FASANENSTRASSE 23
10719 BERLIN
TEL. 030 887 2860
WWW.LITERATURHAUS-BERLIN.DE

CAFÉ-RESTAURANT "WINTERGARTEN"
DAILY FROM 9AM - 12AM

BOOKSTORE
MON. - FRI. 10.30AM - 7.30PM

Some people can read anywhere. Paper or e-book, bright or dark, music or background chatter – none of it matters. Others need absolute quiet, focussed light, legs up, and a soft chair with a hard backrest or the other way round. And of course, reading and engaging with literature should be possible anywhere, in a tent or an elevator, in a mountain hut, and certainly also in an underground garage when you suddenly realise that you're stuck and the exit will only open the following morning around 6am, when the custodian shows up in his little aquarium. For people interested in the world of literature beyond a good book, people who like to attend readings,

book presentations, discussions, or symposiums, Germany offers so-called literature houses – incredibly only since the middle of the 1980s – in Berlin, Frankfurt am Main, Munich, and Hamburg, all of them in consistently impressive buildings.

I came across the Berlin one purely by accident when a number of years ago I was meeting someone in front of the Käthe Kollwitz Museum, which is right next door to the Berlin Literaturhaus on Fasanenstrasse. 'It looks like Florence here', I thought, never having been in Florence, mind you. It had to have been the historicist building, which I dutifully looked up. To put it a bit simply and amateurishly

for those not in the know: historicism is an artistic style that recreates or imitates historical styles. So, fundamentally, historical-retro architecture that proclaims: it worked well once, no doubt it will still work now. Think Neo-Classicism, Neo-Baroque. For a time, this proud building, built in 1889 on a side street off the Ku'damm, was both a disco and a brothel (criminal) and got just a hair's breadth away from being demolished for an Autobahn slip road (even more criminal). If you were wondering whether referendums actually bring about change: yes, they save buildings like this one, which today also houses a restaurant and a garden. In this public (but still a little hidden) oasis, every day finds any number of people sitting down for a spell to read the international press or eat. Others skip the culinary and go straight into the Literaturhaus to feed their minds. One thing it is not: a place for popular literature. And that's by design. The director of the Berlin Literaturhaus supports a metropolitan, open-minded audience interested in authors that don't have the easiest time getting media attention. From German novels and short-story collections (as well as those in translation) to biographies and new collected editions, the programme has a wide range; the temporary exhibitions as well as the events calendar can be found on their website.

And even if you only want to stop by for breakfast, you should at least have a look at the beautifully restored stairwell and perhaps still take a peek to see what exhibition is on before going down to the Kohlhaas & Company bookshop. Regardless of how you choose to spend your time at the Literaturhaus, you can be sure that no Autobahn slip road in the world would ever etch itself so powerfully in your memory.

Wedding

One of the City's Most Singular Places

PIANOSALON CHRISTOPHORI
UFERHALLEN
UFERSTRASSE 8
13357 BERLIN
WWW.KONZERTFLUEGEL.COM

One of the things I remember best from my school days is the darkened classroom where we watched the black-and-white film of *Lord of the Flies*. Nor will I ever forget the chemistry lab and the purple liquid that's created when potassium permanganate falls into a container of water. Or biology class where, thanks to Konrad Lorenz, his rubber boots, and a cackling gaggle of small wild geese, we learned so much about the conditioning of animals. And those concerts that would take place every now and again in the lecture hall. They'd push the concert piano up onto the podium, an Asian-looking woman would adjust her seat, smooth out her

dress, sit down, and let loose. I don't know a lot about classical music. When I hear the word sonata, the first thing I think of is a sleek South Korean car. This high-culture deficit is my mark of Cain, but I have learned not to powder it over any more. In the end, the message arrives, the emotion, the virtuosity. The intensity of certain classical music always reaches me, so a while ago I immediately accepted a friend's invitation to accompany him to a concert in the Pianosalon. I expected dark wood, old coffered walls, and heavy velvet, most likely somewhere in Charlottenburg. Our destination, however, was the Uferhallen in Wedding, right by Ge-

sundbrunnen, names that sound confusingly like linen bedsheets and crisp clear spring water. The reality is much rawer. We found ourselves standing on the premises of the former central workshop of the BVG (the Berlin Transport Company). A nervous streetlight flickered between the asphalt and rubbish, and a strong snow shower chased us into a loft-like hall with an incomparable atmosphere, filled with visitors of every age. Historical instruments hung (and hang) on the walls among numerous pictures. The photos and sculptures were lit by living-room lamps, the seating rows consisted of about 200 chairs – donated and picked up here and there – in just about any colour you could imagine, and on the small stage were one or two of the pianos that started it all. Many years ago, Christoph Schreiber, then still a medical student, began to restore and collect historical concert pianos. As they grew in number, he had to rent rooms in order to keep them all. In the meantime, the piano-fan and family-man had begun working as a neurologist at the trauma hospital in Marzahn. His work was meaningful and time-consuming, but one day Schreiber decided to follow his great passion for chamber music and began organising concerts so his restored treasures could come to some use. Ever since then there has been the Pianosalon Christophori, ever since then Schreiber has given every other week of his life to chamber music, the rest of his time to neurology. This is the condensed origin story of a cultural institution that is unique in Germany, and probably the whole world. Schreiber constantly manages to bring in-ternational stars to Wedding for concerts that would otherwise only take place at the Philharmonie. There are close to 180 musical evenings every year, entry is affordable to all, and on some evenings it is even pay-what-you-want. When things go well, Schreiber can recoup his operating costs with the entrance fees and manage to pay the artists a mini-fee which basically covers their expenses. The reservation system on Pianosalon's website is fair and non-bureaucratic.

The Pianosalon enriches this city unlike anything else. And many people are deeply worried by the fact that the listed Uferhallen complex – home to a large number of artists' studios and the unusual restaurant Der Pförtner (The Porter) in addition to the Pianosalon – was sold for almost €30 million to an investment group in 2017. For the time being, the future is uncertain. There are places that need to be protected. Christoph Schreiber's Pianosalon is definitely one of them.

Drinks Inside the Volcano

BASALT BAR
UTRECHTER STRASSE 38
13347 BERLIN
TUE. - SAT. BEGINNING AT 7PM

My relationship with alcohol varies. People who don't like beer or wine, whose faces freeze in a grimace for minutes after drinking a small schnapps, and who only drink gin-and-tonics because they taste like lemonade are not necessarily predestined to regularly go to bars. Or to put it another way: if a bar could talk, it would lead me to the exit by my ears and say, 'It's definitely time for you to go home.' So for me to enjoy spending time at a bar, it must have a particular flair, a kind of magnetism that attracts me and keeps me there. It can be the light, the people at and behind the bar, or the pictures on the wall – precisely those things that create a good atmosphere.

I fell in love with this place immediately.

The Basalt Bar didn't have to vie for clientele for very long after its March 2016 opening. Whoever discovers it returns. The guests are a good mix of neighbours and visitors; there aren't any posers or loud drinkers. The Utrechter Strasse is in a typical old Berlin neighbourhood. A few shops, some late-night cornershops, nurseries, empty storefronts, re-development projects. Curious tiles decorate the building outside and in. I wouldn't want those in my bathroom, I think, and walk into a darkly lit microcosm. Basalt. It makes me think of a slate-coloured swatch card. 'Basalt,' the dictionary says, 'is the volcanic equivalent of Gabbro (pluton)'. Aha. And, in fact, the bar really is a bit like what I imagine the inside of a volcano to look like. It all seems stark and minimalist. Botany is an essential element of the design. Sensible lighting accents flowers, flower arrangements, and verdant plants; I could take a thousand photos, and every single one would be a hymn to this bar's aesthetic.

The tiles from the facade reappear at the counter, and that's no mistake: made by a manufacturer in Brandenburg, they establish a connection between outside and inside, while unquestionably fitting the rooms' atmosphere. Everything here seems to have been chosen carefully. The drinks are top-notch, and the bartenders are attentive and funny; no wonder *Mixology*, the bar-culture magazine, described this place as delivering both enrichment and salvation.

The half-Irish owner, Kieran Mac Devitt, has a lot of experience in gastronomy. He knows his neighbourhood; after all, he ran a restaurant nearby for a long time. Conveniently, Kieran lives in the rear building, as does the man responsible for the concept: Kieran's business partner, Matthias Heumeier – they've known each other since primary school.

The menu changes about four times a year, in accordance with what is seasonally available. Herbs and other ingredients are chosen with care, the syrups are homemade. Among guests' favourite drinks is the Basilisc, made with basil, French vodka, St. Germain elderberry liquor, fresh lemon, and, naturally, cloudy apple juice. You could try to make one yourself, but believe me: it will taste much better on the spot.

Buenos Aires in the Capital

The tango is a direct expression of something that poets have often tried to state in words: the belief that a fight may be a celebration.

–Jorge Luis Borges

'Wedding is up and coming', one of Berlin's mantras, immediately came to mind when I drove to Gerichtstrasse for a shoot in 2013. At that point, the former Stadtbad indoor pool was still filled with ateliers and good spirits, and, once I actually began to have a look around the street and took in the atmosphere, I realised the metamorphosis of this part of town had been underway for a long time; I just hadn't noticed. With all its clubs, ateliers, and

TANGOLOFT
GERICHTSTRASSE 23, 2ND ENTRANCE
13347 BERLIN
PROGRAMME AND OPENING TIMES:
WWW.TANGOLOFT-BERLIN.DE
ADMISSION FOR *MILONGAS* € 6
COURSES € 10–12 AN HOUR

bars, Lebenshaus Mitte, a large old building with seven separate courtyards, looked like a buzzing beehive. In order to get to know one of the central meeting points of the Berlin tango scene I had an appointment with Mona-Isabelle on the first floor. Berlin: the second-largest tango enclave outside of Buenos Aires. Really? Was a real milonga tango night even possible here among all the graffiti, the crumbling concrete, the urban decay? Hot-blooded passion and steamy heat on a cold grey spring day in Wedding?

Walking into the Tangoloft it was clear: if it's possible, then it will have to be in a place like this. The huge space with its large windows, pictures, flowers, colours, candles, and concert piano already exuded an enormous sensuality. 'It's another world', explained Mona-Isabelle, Tangoloft's director and co-owner since 2007. Here, bathed in colourful light, couples of all ages circled the old wooden floors with great joy and serious expressions, driven by the vigorous rhythms of that particular music. 'Here we place great importance on contemporary tango. Can you hear the difference?' she asked. No, I couldn't. 'No big deal', Mona-Isabelle said. 'For me, it's only important for people to know that what's going on here doesn't have to be nostalgic. Contemporary tango is wonderful.'

The idea for the loft was born in 2001, the brainchild of Henning Klose, a former teacher and tango enthusiast. Ever since the scene in Berlin had begun to swell and milongas grew more professional, he had wanted to create a place which would also be open to improvisation. Neither the elaborate course programme nor the dance clothing on sale in the shop give the impression of being improvised, but the owners have nonetheless been able to conserve the charm of the unfinished in these rooms. Courses take place during the week, starting at 6pm; the Saturday milonga begins at 9pm, and on Sundays it already begins at 3pm. 'And it's over by 10 o'clock?' 'On the contrary', Mona-Isabelle says. 'I can't explain why, but Sundays here stretch on into the bright hours of respectable Monday mornings. Sometimes people even end up being late for work.' I leant back against the wall and watched the dancers. An older man in a white suit came up to me and whispered: 'Women love to be led.' I couldn't nod in agreement and didn't want to laugh, so he quickly added a conciliatory '...when dancing, Madame! May I?' Agreed. I let myself be led, or, well, as best I could. Our feet collided a few times, but he elegantly ignored it. I allowed myself to be flexible but didn't understand a thing about the dance. One thing I did understand though: tango doesn't court you, it grabs you. And if you want to get to know it, this is the best place in Berlin.

Boating for Perfect Summer Days

**FISCHERPINTE: BOAT RENTAL
AM PLÖTZENSEE
NORDUFER 23
13351 BERLIN
TEL. 030 452 4021
SAT. - SUN. 10AM - 9PM,
MON. - FRI. 12PM - 9PM**

Describing certain people as characters can be a bit presumptuous, because who are you to judge? Not to mention that it often sounds a little sarcastic or even borderline mean.

Still, when an unusual person is standing in front of you, you know it – and Monika, the owner of the Fischerpinte at the Plötzensee boathouse, is a special person in a lot of respects, a real character. She wears her heart on her sleeve, her hair in a soft bun, her nails are brightly coloured and decorated, and when the sun comes through the small window and hits the countless rhinestones on her t-shirt, it breaks across her ample bosom in a thousand pris-

matic fragments. She came here for the first time in 1958, she says in a thick Berlin accent. 'I was seven, with my folks. Back then it still was called punting. Didn't cost much: into the boat then back out.' In 1990, she and her husband took over the small tavern and the boat rentals. 'The Wall opened up, and we came here.' In addition to daily fishing permits (starting at € 35), there are 25 skiffs and paddleboats (starting at € 8), soft drinks, spirits, beer, and snacks.

On a summer day like today, the atmosphere corresponds to what a well-paid set-designer would put together for a new soft-drink commercial. Almost all the tables and chairs are taken. Mostly young women and men of various backgrounds casually sitting around the water in shorts and t-shirts, eating snacks and *Buletten* (meat balls), sipping from their glasses, and squinting happily into the sun.

In online travel guides, visitors to this waterside oasis refer to it as a well-kept secret and seem unsure if they should even mention the small hideout at all. Monika, this much is clear, isn't opposed. More people would be welcome, as Wedding, for 45 years *her* Wedding, has noticeably changed. And not necessarily to its benefit. Those new residents running away from Prenzlauer Berg don't bother her as much as those 'who don't have any respect for other people's property.' They often leave their trash lying in the park or climb over the fence at night and cause damage.

But she couldn't envision her life without this place on the lake, even when sometimes she's reached her limit. Monika reaches for her smartphone. With her incredibly long, brightly lacquered nails she moves back and forth across the screen. 'Man, where is it ... I just had it. Ah, here. Whaddya think? Is that a sunset or what? That was yesterday.' She shows me a photo of the Plötzensee that looks like she spiked my drink with LSD earlier. 'I might not have that much strength left for all of this here any more, but when I see something like this, I'm happy.' Monika's eyes grow damp. As if I'd caught her, she quickly looks out the window towards the sun and takes a long drag off her cigarette.

Moabit

Tarantino's Favourite Restaurant

In the past, things had their order: wild hair was considered unkempt; walls had wallpaper and were never not plastered; and of course you didn't have holes in your trousers, why would you? Then came the whole second-hand trend: used clothing and furniture were acclaimed for their special charm, and hand-me-downs were a good argument for sustainability. All well and good, but then someone came up with this shabby chic or tarnished look, and things began to lie to us. Straight out of the factory, objects were furnished with traces of wear to suggest a past that never happened. The perfect machine-scratched enamel tub

ERGUN'S FISCHBUDE
LÜNEBURGER STRASSE 382
10557 BERLIN
TEL. 030 397 5737
DAILY 3PM – 11PM

painted the colour of rust is soulless. Its true sister stood under an apple tree in Paris or Peine for 40 years, served as a washtub, briefly hosted a Christmas carp, and was eventually turned into a planter, rust and all. Here the well-worn word authenticity comes into play. You just can't construct certain things, they have to grow and come together on their own.

And that's the only explanation for how a place like Ergun's Fischrestaurant came to be what it is: a unique place that underwent certain things to grow into its current manifestation. No one here ever said: 'Hey, let's open a dark restaurant in a rough space below the S-Bahn tracks with pieces of paper hanging from the walls and ceiling. You know, to create the feeling of having wandered into a Dadaist collage.' At the beginning of the 1990s, no one was thinking about a restaurant. Ergun Çentibas, Berlin's first Turkish fish trader, used the space for storage. Eventually he had a few market stands on the Maybachufer, at the Crelle market, and in Wedding. At some point, someone brought a second chair to the storage space, and they sat down together to plan out the day. The next time they did, Ergun and his friends decided to prepare some fish for themselves. More chairs arrived, then more tables, more fish, and more people. Then, in 1994, Ergun opened his restaurant, which, by the way, you can enter from two different sides. The menu is as good as fixed: there are a couple kinds of fish (the public's fave is the gilthead seabream for €14, served with a tasty salad for €3.50), a good selection of prawns, and a few Turkish wines. And there are cards hanging from the ceiling. Once price tags for the fish, over time they have become estranged from their original use. It started with one and then more and more showed up. Whether simple thanks for a good meal, sadness over the elimination of a football team from a tournament, or an apology to a wife – Ergun's cards offer a complete sociogram of life. In the corner of the restaurant there is a TV being fed by a video or a DVD player. Whenever I've been there it has shown images of bays. Nothing but bays, a few minutes of the same bay, then the next. Sun, sky, sea. On the tables: glass plates. Beneath the glass plates: further messages from happy guests. 'An unforgettable evening!' and next to it something in Japanese.

Since 2014, Ergun's daughter Mine has run the restaurant. 'We've got a lot of regulars', Mine says. Parliamentarians, state prosecutors, 'and they're all totally chill. German guests are the best, you can quote me on that.' Why? 'Well, life is often chaotic, sometimes your head is really full. And here the forks and knives don't match, the chairs don't match one another or the table, but people have fun.' And they do, you can feel it. In summer, you can also sit outside, but that's almost a shame, for if you do, you'll miss the opportunity to discover something new.

An Unusual Launderette Where Neighbours Meet

FREDDY LECK SEIN WASCHSALON
GOTZKOWSKYSTRASSE 11
TEL. 030 509 16 652
DAILY FROM 7AM – 11PM
WWW.FREDDY-LECK-SEIN-WASCHSALON.DE

Let's make one thing clear right away: Dirk Martens' passion and care for his washing machines has nothing to do with objectophilia.

Surely you've heard about it at some point: people fall in love with a bridge, an object, or the Berlin Wall and strike up a relationship with said object. Take, for example, the American archer Erika Aya Eiffel, who, in the presence of her friends, officially married the Eiffel Tower. Though the authorities did not recognise the marriage, they did not stand in the way of her changing her name. Living together under one roof, however, might remain a bit problematic.

The deep feelings that actor Dirk

Marten harbours for his washing machines (and he does) have nothing to do with that. They come from a sincere sense of gratitude and joy.

Like many good stories, his too began with a small tragedy. Once, in Cologne, there lived a person whom Dirk loved more than anything else and whose biggest dream was to have their own laundrette. '"Right", I said, "then that is what you'll have." Totally naïve of me, it was really expensive. Then out of the blue our love disappeared, and there I was with a laundrette.' After three years, he sold the business, thinking he'd transfer a new and unique concept to Berlin. He found an empty storefront, deco-

rated, no, furnished it, and gave it the name Freddy Leck. 'I thought it would be cool for a launderette owner to have to sign everything "F. Leck" (spot in German). That was the best idea I ever had.' True. The most varied people come here: singles and couples, construction workers and academics, men and women. Some people do their own laundry and pass the time at one of the comfortable tables having a coffee (a latte macchiato costs € 1.90) and a piece of cake (€ 1.20), sometimes working on their laptops or reading the paper, others drop off their laundry and have it delivered to their home smelling fresh and ironed. Freddy Leck's range of services encompasses almost everything that has to do with laundry. Along the wall stand 27 washing machines, they spin and buzz and make Dirk Martens' eyes shine. 'What do you see in these machines that I don't?' I ask him. 'First and foremost, gratitude: they've taken on truly tough work. Then there's gazing through the bull's eye as the laundry spins, watching the dirty water get pumped away until the fresh new water comes. The moment you open the machine and take out all that clean, fresh-smelling laundry. It's incredible.' When you see it that way, it all seems understandable, and what's more: philosophical. It's no accident that the Greek word *katharsis* means purification. I get it. With its colours, patterns, and furniture, sitting in this laundrette is like being on a stage set. In the end, the ideal hotspot for crazy Berliners to spend their time. Dirk Mertens' eyes narrow into a serious look. 'We're all kinds of things, just not crazy. This isn't a hip store. On the contrary, we're dyed-in-the-wool conservatives. If everything's not clean and running smoothly, then you won't like me at all.' I believe him immediately. All the same, he is endlessly funny and friendly. When he's in front of the camera for a shoot, his co-worker Ines takes over the shop with just as much joy and seriousness. Just recently Mertens spent a few days in Japan, but not for a shoot. He opened a Freddy Leck salon in Tokyo because the Japanese are just crazy about him and his products. If you happen to find yourself far from home and you've splashed your shirt with soy sauce, the Tokyo branch is located at 1-3-13 Chuo-cho, Meguro-ju.

1990s Alternative Cinema

FILMRAUSCHPALAST
KULTURFABRIK MOABIT
LEHRTER STRASSE 35
10557 BERLIN
TEL. 030 394 4344

FILMS DAILY AT 6PM, 8PM, AND 10PM
PROGRAMME AND TICKETS AT
WWW.FILMRAUSCH.DE
WWW.KULTURFABRIK-MOABIT.DE/KUFA

In a city full of existentialists, careerists, anarchists, fatalists, lobbyists, utopists, and start-up-ists there really still are a few idealists. People who regularly do things that are not just in their own interests, but in support of a larger idea from which many can profit.

The Kulturfabrik, a stone's throw away from the Hauptbahnhof central train station, is kept alive by such people. Their drive may be fed by a lot of things, but not by commercial interests. In 1991, they occupied the proud building, which had been empty since 1973, bringing together students, local residents, and artists to found four associations and give the old building a new

goal: the area's social and cultural revival. They did it on a volunteer basis and continue to do so today. Here, people dance, party, discuss, exhibit, present, and play music. There are table-football tournaments and theatre performances. And what sadly only a small percentage of Moabit residents know: the Kulurfabrik also has the only cinema in the whole area – the endearing Filmrauschpalast. Three different films are shown every day: at 6pm, 8pm, and 10pm. Tickets cost € 6. Even though the cinema is equipped with the latest digital technology (DCP), you can regularly enjoy films on 35mm, good old analog in other words, earning it the cineas-tes' seal of approval. On Friday and Saturdays during the summer, there's also an open-air cinema (90 seats), entry is free; if it rains, screenings are moved inside, where there are 45 seats. There is no minimum of visitors: if you are the only guest at a screening, then it means you're the only guest: lights out, the film begins. The Filmrausch café is like a mixture of a kitchen in a group flat and a living room, it serves drinks and snacks, and on cold days the powerful old stove gives off a pleasant warmth.

It's exciting to see how and whether this refuge will change, for just a few metres away from the Kulturfabrik a completely new district with the cold name of Europacity is being built on a huge plot of land which has lain fallow for years. It is supposed to contain 1400 apartments, offices, and shops. Nowadays in Berlin it is almost considered good form to be sceptical about such things. How these structural changes will affect the social mix in this already rather mixed area will only be seen once the cranes disappear. But seeing as that among all this city's 'ists' there are also still a few optimists, an establishment like the Kulturfabrik could indeed benefit from its new neighbours. And the other way round.

Readings, Drinks, And Table-Football Tournaments

KAPITEL 21
LEHRTER STRASSE 55
10557 BERLIN
TEL. 030 513 04 910
TUE. - SUN. FROM 6PM
WWW.KAPITEL21.DE

When I moved to Berlin at the end of the 1990s, there wasn't yet any talk of a tight housing market. Coming from Hamburg, where people lost many nights of sleep after being offered to view an apartment with 50 other people ('The real estate agent called me back! I'm flipping out. Drinks on me!'), I was traumatised and couldn't believe my luck when I saw all the offers for reasonable apartments in the newspapers' heavy weekend editions. At that time, I almost moved to Moabit (130 square-metres, four rooms, turn-of-the century building, 750 marks, electricity included). In retrospect it was good that it didn't work out, for Moabit and I, well, for various reasons we just

didn't become friends back then. In the meantime, things have changed, just like so many things always change in this city.

In addition to the old established Moabit residents, there are now also a lot of young families, students from all over the world, creative types, uncreative types, third-generation migrants, and representatives of all generations. Everything is there, a turbulent mix distributed across 112 streets. The time of ridiculously low rents is gone here though, just like in most of the rest of Berlin. In the rehabbed buildings, the upper crust is slowly coming into closer contact with welfare recipients, for the most part unwillingly.

Lehrter Strasse is an important thoroughfare in the eastern part of the area. It's not half as bustling as, for example, Turmstrasse, but for that very reason it's all the more beloved, as there are a few interesting destinations on this narrow street to the central train station. In 2012, the Bosnian-born Berliner Asmir opened Kapitel 21 – named after the old Moabit postal code (until 1993, letters were supposed to say '1000 Berlin 21') – across from the Kulturfabrik.

Asmir is actually a musician and producer. He plays electronic music and, with his band, swing. When he first came up with the idea for a place for art exhibitions, readings, concerts, and good drinks, there wasn't much in the area and nothing at all in terms of a space that wanted to be a part of bar culture without being stuffy. The fact that Kapitel 21 has since found its niche and its mixed clientele has to do with the enthusiasm and commitment to quality with which Asmir runs his place. Examples of his enthusiasm are the football table lit from the inside (Kapitel 21 regularly holds tournaments) – and the quality of his drinks. Crafted with only the best ingredients and very little sugar, he makes his own lemonades and syrups for the cocktails, and the team brews its own beer: 'My response to industrial beer, at a normal price and without and hop extract.' Connoisseurs can drink their way through many craft beers and 20 different types of vodka, and if you get peckish, you can order bar food like olives, peanuts, nachos, or Asmir's vegan pasta salad. 'I make it with mushrooms, paprika, sun-dried tomatoes, and hot peppers. It's great! You want a plate?' Absolutely.

Berlin's Oldest Pastry Shop

KONDITOREI BUCHWALD
BARTNINGALLEE 29
10557 BERLIN
TEL. 030 391 5931
DAILY 9AM – 7PM
WWW.KONDITOREI-BUCHWALD.DE

People who were socialized in the 1970s liked their desserts colourful, sweet, and unmistakable. Back then, a dark-brown plain *Baumkuchen* log had a hard time competing with those creamy or brightly coloured desserts. Raspberry ice cream was artificially fortified with such strong scents and flavours that you could smell it at the other end of the apartment, and the woodruff ice cream was so green that biochemists would no doubt still find the traces of its fluorescent chemicals in my system today. To us kids, Baumkuchen was like political discussions at the coffee table. Boring, dreary. Tactically speaking, not even its rather clever and artful rationing ('Now

everyone, just a tiny little piece, Baumkuchen is expensive') made it any more interesting.

But, as we know, things change. All of a sudden you like coriander or basil, and all of a sudden you also understand: Baumkuchen tastes great.

This delicacy first appeared in a cookbook in the 17th century. Making it was considered costly and complicated: thin sheets of batter were poured layer by layer (like the rings of a tree or *Baum*) onto a spinning cylinder that was spinning horizontally on a – in my words – Dönerkebab-like spit. In order to create the ribbed outer shape, the dough is then tied off at regular intervals with strings. Don't try this one at home.

Baumkuchen continues to be considered a kind of hallmark for the confectioner's guild. And even if you can now buy it at a discounter, it tastes incomparably fresh and good when it is professionally baked – and without any doubt the best is to be had at Buchwald.

This, the oldest pastry shop in Berlin, has existed for more than 160 years, even providing cakes and tarts to the erstwhile Prussian court.

The café is spacious, and in the summer you can sit out on the terrace by the Spree.

You will run into a diverse offering: a breakfast menu, plus various tarts and cakes. By all means take some Baumkuchen to go, you could give it to someone as a gift.

But, and I say this from experience, don't be upset if you end up keeping it for yourself.

Tiergarten

Swath of Green between Schöneberg and Mitte

Driving on the Autobahn in the direction of Berlin, there are two exits marked CITY CENTRE: one in the East (Alexanderplatz) and one in the West (Zoo Station). Now, being a Schönebergerin, my gaze already naturally leans towards the West, but, to my eyes, the true centre of the city really does lie just a little bit to the left of the geographical centre: namely, in the Grosser Tiergarten. Don't get confused: in this context the word *Tiergarten* is no synonym for the zoo. My Tiergarten is a park which – like a crispy chocolate that's hard to break up into equal pieces – is made up of a number of odd-sized large spaces that belong together but are crisscrossed here

GROSSER TIERGARTEN

and there by a few streets. One of those is the Strasse des 17. Juni: known to tourists for the Victory Column and the flea market, to Berliners for its nerve-racking closures and speed cameras.

The park is 210 hectares large. Originally conceived of as the private hunting grounds for the electors of Brandenburg, its enclosures were torn down in the middle of the 18th century at the behest of Frederick the Great, who opened it to the public as a so-called *Lustpark*. Rightfully so. After World War II, hunger and cold were the order of the day. Most of the park's close to 200,000 trees were dug up and used as firewood. On the newly levelled grounds, people planted anything and everything that could grow and be somewhat filling. Reforestation was begun in 1949, and Berlin, that ragged problem child, allowed itself to be given a lot of gifts: over 250,000 young trees were donated from various cities in Germany, and during the Berlin Blockade all the new greenery reached its home by plane.

Ever since I got my dog, foregoing my daily ride through the Tiergarten has become inconceivable. Some days I feel like I'm the only person there, I don't encounter a soul; it's as if I were in the eye of a storm. I once observed a woman who'd brought a parrot cage along and was letting her two birds hop around on a tree. Sometimes you run into groups of people practicing laughter or silence, sun worshippers, turtles, raccoons, and even the leather woman, an old gripe in a bikini who lies in the exact same spot in all kinds of wind and weather, reading a paper and yelling at any dog that happens to trot past. Joggers, walkers (including a man who walks backwards), picnics, and, on summer Sundays, a group of old Portuguese people who sit on folding chairs around little tables and play cards. And – for the record – only one time in almost 10 years did I witness a man jump out from behind an oak and shake his privates at me. I was so enraged that I shouted: 'You goddamn exorcist!' A few metres later I thought, 'Well, OK. There are a few advantages to all those sex and porn sites online: people stay at home.' I hadn't had to use the word exhibitionist for a long time. It had obviously left my mind.

A Touch of the Baltic in Prussia

TEAHOUSE IN THE ENGLISH GARDEN
RESTAURANT AND BEER GARDEN
ALTONAERSTRASSE 2
10557 BERLIN
TEL. 030 394 80 400
TUE. - SAT. FROM 12PM, SUN. FROM 10AM
WINTER OPENING TIMES
WWW.DAS-TEEHAUS.JIMDO.COM

'Nitwit!', 'What ya' lookin' at, you stuck-up fool?', 'Watch yourself, big man, before I crack you one' – in Berlin there's a lot of snapping and growling but rarely any biting. In principle, Berliners like to work themselves up. There sure are enough reasons. You get angry about construction sites (in mathematical terms, every 53 metres), state visits that lead to street closures and endless red lights, and demonstrations, of which, on average, there are nine a day. You get passionately worked up about tourists, bus drivers, taxi drivers, cyclists, drivers, and pedestrians. All of which are naturally the enemies of every other group, it's a given. But if there is one thing that leads

to collective anger it's the closure of the Strasse des 17. Juni, which with its width of 85.2 metres is the widest street in the city. There's always something: the open-air football viewings, fashion week, the marathon. When this boulevard, which stretches from Ernst-Reuter-Platz out west to the Brandenburg Gate, is blocked from Grosse Stern onwards, it leads to massive traffic jams. You might think the city must have gotten used to it, but I assure you it hasn't. All the same, there's a kind of preventative therapy to be found at www.ist diestrassedes17tenjunigesperrt. de, which documents the closings, making it an ideal bookmark for choleric types and trav-

ellers who have to make it to the train station on time.

Be that as it may, during one of those very closures I decided to relocate my dog's walk into the part of the Tiergarten that had until then always seemed too small: the bit between Bellevue Palace and the Hansaviertel neighbourhood, the so-called English Garden, which got its name thanks to the gifts of plants that Berlin received from England after the war and that also significantly contributed to the reforestation of this part of the Tiergarten.

Just a few steps into the English Garden, you come across the most unusual sight (well, as far as the capital is concerned): a neat, symmetrically laid garden with benches, flowerbeds, and a touch of Baden-Baden, all leading up to a large, thatched-roof house. As if a helicopter had lifted up a roomy cottage from the Baltic resort of Sylt and accidentally dropped it in Berlin. In all these years I had never noticed this place before. People were lying about on the grass, relaxing, reading, napping, or talking. If you're hungry, you can go to the restaurant or have a seat on the teahouse's huge terrace and order a snack, a salad, or some cake. During the summer, they fire up a large grill. On Sundays, there are free live concerts with two bands each time. In winter, of course, the open-air events disappear, but after going for a walk you can still come to sit around the fireplace and enjoy a hot cup of tea. Just don't come in January or February, then the teahouse is closed.

Scandi-national Representation

THE NORDIC EMBASSIES IN BERLIN
RAUCHSTRASSE 1
10787 BERLIN
TEL. 030 50 500
MON. - FRI. 10AM - 7PM,
SAT. - SUN. 11AM - 4PM
CANTEEN: MON. - FRI. 10AM - 4PM
WWW.NORDISCHEBOTSCHAFTEN.ORG

Consumer culture, underpayment, mass production, price dumping, disastrous working conditions, loss of quality: allow me to put these terms out there. In our age of globalisation, so many things are not transparent or fair, but cheap and dubious. I admire anyone who can radically alter their relationship to consumption: up till now, I've only managed small things. All the same, it's got to be said: many years ago, two large companies, global players, helped us Germans to have more choice and taste, freeing us from all the mustiness and monotony of boring identical products. It was the Swedes. They brought us more attractive, affordable furniture

and more interesting clothes, and that's a fact.

In terms of quality of life, education, gender equality, and design, the northern countries can generally be considered tasteful pioneers and ambassadors. This is also evident in the embassies at the southern end of the Tiergarten. As an expression of solidarity, the Swedes, Icelanders, Danes, Finns, and Norwegians bundled together their diplomatic representation under one roof. The five embassy buildings, each designed by architects from their own country, are connected to the Fellehues, a shared space that also has a restaurant. The Fellehues is open to the public and welcomes all, whether Berlin-

er or tourist. On one of the outer walls, stylishly designed large banners announce the exhibitions and events currently taking place there.

Under the 'Book of the Month' heading, they publicise the works of Nordic writers; there are regular concerts in what's known as the 'jazz canteen'; and they offer a lectures and discussions on a wide range of themes and subjects. The coffee bar on the first floor is open weekdays from 8.30am to 4.30pm, weekends between 11am and 3.30pm. An insider's tip: up on the third floor there's the international canteen, which offers three different dishes every day; there's always a vegetarian option, and the fresh-fish option is almost a point of honour. On warm days you can have your meals and/or drinks on the large terrace outside. If you plan to come here on a week-day, however, do pay attention to the times, as between 11.30 and 1pm all tables are reserved for the embassy workers. But before or after, you are welcome to have a seat.

A Hymn to Architecture

THE PREGNANT OYSTER:
HAUS DER KULTUREN DER WELT
JOHN-FOSTER-DULLES-ALLEE 10
10557 BERLIN
TEL. 030 397 870
DAILY 10AM - 7PM
PROGRAMME AT WWW.HKW.DE

Alex, a good friend, had taken me along to a party at the Pregnant Oyster. I was heartbroken and feeling bad. How could my ex-boyfriend fall in love again so quickly? And who was she? Alex was in exactly the same situation: his former girlfriend was also talking about true love with her ominous new guy. While everyone around us that evening was busy dancing and laughing, we sat pitiful and still beside the loudspeakers, drinking schnapps with heavy eyes and yelling sad stories into each other's ears. Two wretched figures, a pathetic display of heartbreak. Then all of a sudden I noticed him in the crowd, my ex, his arm slung around a woman, and soon they

were making their way towards us. 'What should I say, Alex? Help!' But Alex just heavily laid his pale head on my shoulder and closed his eyes. 'Oh no,' he whispered. Then everything went rather quickly. 'Hey.' 'Hey. No way! You guys know each other? Crazy. We're going to go dance. See you later.' It was truly an encounter of the third kind: out of 3 million other Berliners, our exes had fallen in love with each other. What a truly bizarre meeting.

So my premier visit was a disaster, but already on my second I was able to more justly appreciate the Pregnant Oyster. Let's begin this way: I like this building from all sides and from all angles.

Architecturally it has been described as a landmark of western modernity. Erected in 1957, the building was, labelled a convention hall and functioned as the US contribution to the International Building Exhibition (INTERBAU). Since 1989, it has been known as the 'House of World Cultures' (HKW). It is located next to the Federal Chancellery, directly on the river Spree, and is surrounded by green areas and trees, with a large terrace on its upper deck and a massive terrace by the water. The pleasure boats chug by, and if you suddenly get the urge to go aboard, the jetty is just a few metres away. According to its self-description the HKW 'creates a forum for the contemporary arts and critical debates'. Here you will find conventions, conferences, festivals, lectures, and exhibitions dedicated to almost any social, cultural, and scientific concern you can think of. Often the topics are exciting, even if the announcements leave me somewhat perplexed. What exactly is it about? Could you reformulate that, please? If you are undaunted by convoluted and overly intellectual content, no doubt you will encounter some highly interesting events.

West Berlin's Oldest Secret

CAFÉ AM NEUEN SEE
LICHTENSTEINALLEE 2
10787 BERLIN
TEL. 030 254 4930
DAILY 9AM – 12AM
WWW.CAFEAMNEUENSEE.DE

If I were rich, I would rent out the Café am Neuen See every year for 24 hours just to throw a big party – yes, here in this at first glance plain-looking single-storey bungalow with the panorama windows and the immense beer garden in the middle of the city. People walking around the Tiergarten would hear the music and the cheerful laughter of partying women above the deep mumbling of the party's urbane dancers, and draw closer to my fluttering caution tape in order to cast a glance at this unique place on the water. A few tourists would stand around and say, 'Did you hear that? They really know how to party, they sound like animals!' and a pas-

ser-by would answer, 'Yes, they do. But the scream you just heard came from the zoo, it's nearby.' A young Japanese woman or an Inuit would try to snap a picture of the crane perched on one of the skiffs lapping at the pier. If it was winter, they'd have built the little structure they put up every year, so my red-cheeked guests could try their hand at curling or just warm their hands at one of the fireplaces, before going back inside to order one of many varieties of wafer-thin, wagon-wheel-sized pizza, soft in the middle with large bubbles in the crust. A few of my guests would grab some chairs and push them over to one of the four fireplaces so that they could look into the fire. But most likely it'd be summer, so that we could all sit outside, gently lit by the innumerable strings of lights hanging from the old trees like garlands. A few sparrows would come to the tables and rather daringly pick off the odds and ends left on the plates. If I were rich, all of this would happen, but this is probably the case for everyone who comes to find this place. The restaurant is open the entire year; the large beer garden with its white veal sausage, leberwurst, potato salad, pizza, salad, and drinks of course closed during the winter. To tell the truth, this place really isn't all that much of a secret any more, and wasn't 25 years ago either. Let's call it a classic you seek out to start off the quiet part of the day or glide off on the ponds in a skiff. If you park a few metres away or want to walk a bit, you'll find yourself at the outer enclosures of the zoo. So don't be afraid if from around the corner a lama suddenly winks at you.

45

U1 / U2 / U3 / U4 NOLLENDORFPLATZ, U1 KURFÜRSTENSTRASSE

Vienna's Love Child

CAFÉ EINSTEIN STAMMHAUS
KURFÜRSTENSTRASSE 58
10785 BERLIN
TEL. 030 263 9190
DAILY 8AM – 12AM
WWW.CAFEEINSTEIN.COM

There are 118 places named Berlin throughout the world. And nevertheless only a few people would unintentionally get off the train in Chad or Papua New Guinea if they had a ticket to Berlin. Here the popular name of the German capital allows little ground for misunderstanding. Berlin's multitude of identical streetnames is another story though. By my count there are nine Charlotten, Linden, and Parkstrassen; you will find eight Kirch, Bahnhofs, Garten, and Goethestrassen on the map; and there are many other examples.

Keep that in the back of your head for any future appointments. And don't forget that there are also a number of cafés

and restaurants with the same names. It's extremely confusing. I bring this up because, back when I was new to Berlin, I once had an appointment at Café Einstein. The minutes passed and no one came. In those days before everyone had a mobile you just had to wait, it was awful. The man who was supposed to meet me was waiting in the Café Einstein on Unter den Linden, while I was in the Café Einstein on Kurfürstenstrasse. We each thought the other person was not reliable and certainly not in love, so the romance ended before it even began.

In the meantime, Café Einstein has long been a franchise, which means that there are numerous shops throughout the city with the same name. One of my favourite places in Berlin, however, is the Café Einstein Stammhaus in Tiergarten. It was opened in 1978 as a typical Viennese coffeehouse, while at the same time functioning as a restaurant. The villa, built in 1878 in a Neo-Renaissance style, has a wild past. In the 1920s, it housed a secret gambling club where members of the Weimar Republic's high society, as befitting their social status, let it rip with champagne, cigars, and caviar. During the time of the Nazis, an SS agency moved in and had the villa's Jewish owners removed; two *Stolpersteine* (literally 'stumbling stones') have been placed before the entrance in their memory. As paradoxical as it sounds: the villa managed to come through the war's bombings unscathed, but almost did not survive the years after. For a long time, the house was empty and in danger of collapse until an Austrian in exile decided to bring Viennese coffeehouse culture to Berlin. In the large, salon-like rooms' dignified atmosphere, black-and-white-clad waiters drift across the old oak parquet serving sumptuous breakfast, fluffy wiener schnitzel, and fragrant apple strudel.

During the summer, the garden is open to guests, and if you come in the evening you should definitely have a look in the Lebensstern. That's the name of the upstairs bar with wood-covered walls and leather club chairs, where you can choose between 150 types of gin and close to 600 types of rum. Incidentally, there are also tons of different brandies to help you digest the top-notch Kaiserschmarrn dessert you enjoyed downstairs a little earlier.

46

U1 KURFÜRSTENSTRASSE

One of Europe's Finest Hat Shops

HAT STORE FIONA BENNETT
POTSDAMER STRASSE 81-83
10785 BERLIN
TEL. 030 280 96 330
MON. - SAT. 10AM - 7PM
WWW.FIONABENNETT.DE

It must have been around 1990 or so when I got to know my good friend Sabine. Following a TV broadcast, my team and I were invited to the apartment of Wolfgang Flatz, a really kind and crazy action painter and provocateur who, for example, once had himself hung upside down in a former synagogue to be used as a bell clapper – a unique performance, but quite typical for him. In any event, as part of an installation of his, Sabine was majestically sat on a throne in a sweeping costume made out of unused rubbish bags, benevolently nodding and waving to visitors. As 'the queen', she was part of the laid-back and inspiring Berlin scene that made the

sights into her life, Fiona's autobiography, *Vom Lockern der Federn* (On loosening your feathers), at the same time functions as a chronicle of the wild years before and after the fall of the Wall. In the here and now, British-born Bennett is probably the best and most successful milliner in the country. Her internationally known creations are legendary. Even Hollywood stars know her name: famous personalities like Brad Pitt and Christina Aguilera have made their way to this very particular shop, where any visitor feels like they've found themselves on the set of an opulent French film. Or made their way into a very aesthetically pleasing foreign head. Or someone else's fantasy. Be it simple or outrageous, Fiona never simply presents her creations in an attractive way – she always immediately outlines the bigger artistic picture as well. She has a particular feel for colours and forms, and uses only the best materials. Take a look at her store; from the outside you can also see into the workshop. And right across the street is the Wintergarten variety theatre. In its basement restrooms you once again feel like you've stepped into some kind of fantasy or film set, for it is there that Fiona Bennett, together with her partner Hans-Joachim

walled city into a cell full of crazies – every day there were unusual happenings, concerts, and fashion shows. Imagination and a talent for improvisation grew in direct proportion to the lack of money.

One of the greatest driving forces of this time was the milliner Fiona Bennett, whom Sabine one day introduced me to. Looking like Snow White in her pageboy cut, she was charismatic, creative, elegant, and warm-hearted. It is impossible to enumerate how many spectacular events she initiated and furnished, all the people she brought together, or all the fashion, art, and music concepts she realised alone or in a team. Providing deeper in-

Böhme, has once more created a unique little cosmos. A stage set you walk into that stuns you into amazement. In the best of cases with a brand-new hat on your head, of course.

Prenzlauer Berg, Friedrichshain

An Extremely Unusual Hair Salon

FRANK UND AMANDA
RODENBERGSTRASSE 6
10439 BERLIN
TEL. 030 411 98 078
MON., WED., FRI. 8AM - 10PM

Whenever we're looking for a new dentist, gynaecologist, mechanic, or hair stylist, we like to rely on the suggestions and experiences of knowledgeable friends – a reliable system. At this point it's too late to ask Prince for the number of a good hairstylist, unfortunately, but you could still go talk to Rammstein or punk legend Nina Hagen. Even if their personal haircuts don't quite reflect your personal taste, a celebrity's recommendation is still a stamp of approval for a certain level of professionality. Frank Conte-Schäfer has stood face to face with the aforementioned stars – and a whole lot of non-celebrities too – or rather, behind them, his scissors in hand. If you

turned back and looked at him, you'd find yourself looking into a friendly face, eyes encircled by a pair of glasses, a few tattoos here and there. The *Tagesspiegel* paper calls him a style icon of the East, which is due to his wild past and maybe even more to the way he sees the world. Born in 1959, Frank comes from a privileged GDR family; his father was a well-known actor. The son, on the other hand, didn't have much interest in the system. Equipped with a powerful imagination, he ducked the expectations directed towards him ('Become a doctor. Or a conductor.') and decided instead to pursue his dream job of being a hairstylist. In 2007, together with his girlfriend Amanda Bethke, he opened his own Salon, which by all means has deserved the capital S. The second you walk through the door, all 85 billion nerve cells of the average human brain begin to fire: 'What's going on in *here*?' The ambience successfully works as a kind of confrontation therapy for any minimalist, as here there is not a single free space, nothing is grey, stark, or at a right angle. This is a mini-museum of Schäfer's life as well as a memorial to many decades of Berlin, to fashion and excess, to fantasies, parties, and gadgets. Photos, shoes, pictures, and puppets are stuck to, or suspended from, the walls and ceiling, in the corners, right, left, up, and down. Unheard of in the entire world. But don't let this turn you off: Frank and Amanda know their profession. Their clients are not freaks (well, there have got to be a few), but people from the neighbourhood, business folks, and regulars who have been coming for years and need to be all snazzy and neat so they can work behind a sales or bank counter the very next day. Is there anything he won't do as a stylist? 'Yeah,' Frank says. 'Perms.'

48

Shoes Made to Measure

At the start of my twenties, I developed a platform-shoe phase out of the blue. Whenever I wore them, my legs felt insanely long. The heel was high and wide; I didn't totter but kind of stomped, though naturally I didn't find that to be the case at the time. Sadly, there were as good as no suppliers. I was too late for the 1970s and too early for the 1990s. With a lot of luck I'd find a pair second-hand or at a flea market from time to time. Today I can type 'platform shoes green leather' into a search engine and just a few seconds later receive thousands of offers from Virginia, Bad Salzuflen, and Rio. Before the age of online shopping there were indeed things

SHOEMAKER ANNA RAKEMANN
SCHWEDTER STRASSE 18
10119 BERLIN
FOR APPOINTMENTS:
TEL. 0163 6 620 088 OR
INFO@ANNA-RAKEMANN.DE

yellow and red leather. When we came to pick them up a few days later, they still smelled like fresh glue. Homemade shoes! We were so happy. Back at home we didn't wear them once, not a single time, they were just too red, too yellow, and seemed absurdly misshapen. If we ever decided to have shoes made for us again, they would look different.

And Anna would be the one to make them, that much is a given. Stepping into Anna Rakemann's shop means leaving Prenzlauer Berg's co-working spaces and vegan supermarkets behind. It's amazing how a self-enclosed world can arise in such a little space – Anna is a shoemaker, a modern woman who in the midst of her tools and workshop looks like a timeless painting: the symmetrical face, severe haircut, work apron, her eyes focussed in friendly concentration. The many steps required to create a pair of made-to-measure shoes follow a fascinating choreography. In her hands are the main players: leather, wood, fabric, clamps, knife, glue, thread, and soldering irons. Anna is very good at what she does, and any visitor gets hypnotised watching her work.

Because of her pigeon toes she had to wear orthopaedic shoes as a child, which she didn't like

that simply were not to be had, and you had to make the best of it. One time I went to Bali for a few weeks with my best friend. Driving around bumpy roads on a rusty moped we accidentally discovered Hero, a Balinese shoemaker who showed off his homemade pairs on wobbly wooden roadside shelving. He also had a few orthopaedic examples, which he'd made for the village's oldest man, whose left leg was too short. These left shoes had a massive platform and if Hero could make a 7-centimetre block once, then he would certainly be able to do it again at our behest. We scraped our money together and ordered two pairs of platform shoes in at all, even if they did help her walk. One day, she vowed, she'd make stylish shoes that would also be comfortable. And that is exactly what Anna does today. With great talent and professionality she takes on her client's designs and develops a footbed on the spot. After the initial consultation, she creates a mould and then a sample version before the finished shoe can be picked up.

A woman I got into a conversation with in front of the store told me she had long considered such things to be excessive luxury items. In the meantime, however, she owns three pairs on which she goes 'through life divinely'. She is only angry that she didn't think of it sooner. 'My car regularly gets new tires, meanwhile I'm wobbling about on shoes that pinch my feet. What nonsense.' She has even infected her circle of friends with the bug. For their birthdays they now all ask for money to get a pair of shoes made. One advantage to getting older, at least. In addition to spiritual maturity, of course.

Ice, Ice Baby (and Oh so Healthy)

CALIFORNIA POPS
EBERSWALDER STRASSE 32
10437 BERLIN
CLOSED NOV. – MARCH
12.30PM – 6PM
(WHEN IT'S NICE OUT, LONGER)
WWW.CALIFORNIA-POPS.DE

ADDITIONAL BRANCH IN KREUZBERG
CALIFORNIA POPS
FALCKENSTEINSTRASSE 4
10997 BERLIN

I will never forget the moment my friend Lolly Berkel called me to excitedly shriek into the phone that she had got an ice-cream machine for her birthday. But no matter what we put into that rotating, rattling plastic contraption, all that ever came out was sticky, somewhat cold, and unappealing slush. The thing quickly ended up in the Berkels' basement. A few years ago, when those new omnipotent, extremely expensive kitchen machines came on the market, I was a guest at my former ear doctor's, who in the meantime had begun to offer mindfulness seminars. For dessert he proudly handed out homemade strawberry ice cream without sugar,

milk, or cream, 'very healthy'. It tasted as horrible as old snow, but as I was sitting across from my host I spooned the sour cold mass down my throat with great self-control. Healthy ice cream. Sounds great. Organic, hand-made – wonderful. But let's be honest: it's got to taste good or else none of that means a thing.

And then one day I happened to park my car in front of an ice-cream shop with a window display that looked so enticing and unusual I had to take a photo. I'd never seen those kinds of popsicles before, the variety, the colours, the flavours. 'Ever had one?' the man behind the street counter asked. 'No,' I answered truthfully, 'but we'll change that

right away.' I added money to the meter, rummaged about for my wallet, and decided to work my way right through the whole range. The idea for making this kind of popsicle came to Jörg and Tim, the makers of California Pops, on a trip through South America. The *paletas* there are made of pure ice cream that, thanks to its high percentage of fruit, tastes incomparably good. 'They make it with really fresh ingredients. I don't think they sell any Magnums there. "That's just awesome," we thought, "we need to do that in Berlin."' They now have two shops, and people are constantly beating down their doors. Their homemade ice cream is made from all-natural ingredients; as a general rule, organic products, all-natural yogurt, and either organic or oat milk. They completely forego any preservatives or food colouring. Completely foregoing sugar is impossible, of course, not if it is to taste like it does. Nevertheless, they keep it at an absolute minimum, which you'd never guess judging by the flavour. Now, because it's Berlin there is also a large selection of vegan options in flavours like cucumber, lemon, mango, or strawberry. The only thing that confuses me is that they are so annoyingly delicious. And in case you got the impression that all the options I've praised sound far too reasonable – cucumber, fruit, those flavours all sound like frozen yoga – then I would like to bring the following descriptions to the table: 'cheesecake', 'white chocolate with matcha, or 'cashew with dark chocolate'. Let's go crazy.

When Did You Last Play Billiards?

POOL & CIGARS
SCHÖNHAUSER ALLEE 36
10435 BERLIN
TEL. 030 405 00 436
MON. - FRI. FROM 5PM,
SAT. - SUN. FROM 1PM
WWW.POOLANDCIGARS.DE

For my friend and me, by far the most interesting guy of our youth was 'the Man in Black'. Good, in the 1980s and early 90s, aesthetically problematic times, deciding to wear black was always a safe bet. People sat around on sofas in black PVC, carefully patting the almost immovable contours of their styled hair and toasting one another with black-stemmed Leonardo glasses. Black stood in welcome contrast to the neon gear and all the other fashion curveballs that against all odds are now slouching in the front rows of retro fashion shows again. The Man in Black dressed in suits of the finest threads. With his dark hair combed back from his angu-

lar face, he looked like something between Nick Cave and David Bowie, which put him in a league so supercool that not even we, the somewhat-cool, ever dared to speak to him. That's why we never learned his name, which no doubt just added to the legend, for any name other than Johnny would have killed the mystery. He always came and went alone, to every bar, every club, and every disco, and I always hoped he would like to dance, because his every move seemed infinitely mature and sexy to me. He played billiards with a straight face and won most of the time; anything else would have been simply unimaginable. He fascinated me, the way he scanned the table,

casually rubbed the tip of the cue in the light-blue chalk, elegantly got into position like a jaguar, and then sunk the ball, his head down close to the green felt. Back then I played billiards pretty well myself – I'm talking about the pool variation: six holes, white cue ball, black eight – but I would never have gone up against someone like him. One of the most coveted tables was in a club called Pasta Basta. The rules were clear: the winner remained at the table, every challenger had to put a mark on the edge. If you were unlucky, you got the crooked cue stick, but at least then you had an excuse for any screw-up. When there were a lot of people standing around the table, you automatically either began to play more ambitiously or never got anything right. Then as now there is normally a pleasant silence when people play billiards; it's as if you are watching two actors perform. For people who are interested in either actively or passively enjoying this game again, Pool and Cigars is a good place to do it. The loft-like space exudes something meditative, no doubt due to the background noise, as one ball will be hitting another, *ttklackkkk*, on at least one of the fifteen tables, copper lamps casting warm light on each from above. Fortunately the clientele is mixed: amateurs as well as near pros, women and men, friends and strangers. If you come by yourself, you can take a seat at the bar and take everything in. You won't have any trouble finding a partner to play against.

Pool and Cigars is located on the vast grounds of the Kulturbrauerei, with its wonderful cinemas, the Soda Club, a museum, two theatres, a dance school, and so much more that someone has certainly written a book about it all. A visit is by all means worth it.

Just now I paused a moment when I thought of comparing billiards to chess, the quiet, the concentration, the seriousness, and what came to mind but a quote from Albert Einstein (or attributed to him anyway): 'Billiards is the well-developed art of thinking ahead. It is not only a game, but first and foremost a demanding sport, which requires good stamina, the logical thinking of a chess player, and the stable hand of a concert pianist.'

One more thing: if you happen to be Johnny, please get in touch.

Where the Wall First Fell

BÖSEBRÜCKE
BORNHOLMER STRASSE
10439 BERLIN

If you can recall Michael Jackson's video for "Billie Jean", you will also remember the strange waterfront-y set he walks through, light appearing wherever his shoes touch the ground. If Berlin's pavements could light up at places where important things had happened, the city would be bright indeed, and one of the brightest places would without a doubt be the Bösebrücke on Bornholmer Strasse. It was here on 9 November 1989, when this was a border checkpoint, that the Wall actually first fell, in the form of a boom barrier that countless arms enthusiastically and incredulously raised from a sullen horizontal to an unmistakable vertical. This was the first place the border opened, that border so many people never really wanted.

Prior to this, there had been a press conference presenting new travel regulations that would make it possible for citizens of the GDR to leave the country, but then to please travel back. Günter Schabowski from the Politburo of the SED (the Socialist Unity Party of Germany) routinely and emotionlessly rattled off his speech until a journalist asked when the new regulations would go into effect, and he hopelessly lost his thread. 'To the best of my knowledge ... immediately, without delay.' He was confused; in fact, they were not supposed to go into effect for one more day. The structures were not yet in place, the information had not reached all of those responsible, there was no finished plan. But it was too late. As if Schabowski had opened a bottle of cola that had been violently shaken beforehand, immediately hundreds, soon thousands, of GDR citizens made their way to the border checkpoints. Curious, exhilarated, impatient. Was it really true? Would it still be the same tomorrow? At Bornholmer Strasse, the cluster of people grew larger by the minute. The border soldiers tried to bring the situation under control with words, which in retrospect is still incredible, because everyone there knew that despite the general euphoria they still had orders to shoot. Would one of the soldiers lose their nerves and shoot into the crowd? Some people sang, some climbed up onto the 'Anti-Fascist Protection Rampart' (as the Wall was officially known), others helped each other up then slid back down or suddenly found themselves sitting up on top. The way things went is by now well known, but that it began here is a bit less so, and that's why there are information panels with photos and texts northeast of the Bösebrücke, arranged in a permanent open-air exhibition that is open to all. On every anniversary of that November evening an ecumenical memorial service takes place at this former border checkpoint.

If you happen to find yourself here: carefully cross the street to the other side of the bridge and look south across the countless tracks. Wide vistas like this aren't all that common in Berlin.

A Patchwork of Wild Locations

RAW GELÄNDE
REVALER STRASSE 99
10245 BERLIN

On my first visit to the RAW grounds I felt like I had slipped into a kaleidoscope, incidentally an extremely appealing prospect. A lot of the huge grounds of the former royal Prussian railway workshop right next to Warschauer Strasse was still under construction, or at least looked that way. Here was a club, there a bar, but it was already clear that once again one of those small Gallic villages had arisen, one created by militant creative types or creative militants who, for the most part, wanted to create something good and unusual. Whatever was there was used, whatever was missing was replaced with something improvised, and almost every corner

ended up glowing under a layer of colourful street-art make-up. After serving as a railway workshop for around 130 years, by the beginning of the new century this area had slowly and defiantly developed into a lively quarter that did not serve any higher ideal, or if it did, then certainly not return or profit maximisation. Nowadays people come here to dance, eat, and drink, walk around, and party. Among other things there's the wonderful street-art gallery Urban Spree with its beer garden, a flea market, clubs like Cassiopeia and the Haubentaucher, the Astra-Kulturhaus, and a skatehall, plus concerts and exhibitions.

Today, the rawness, charm, and flair all remain, but there are other features as well. For a spell the RAW grounds fell on hard times: muggings, assaults, drug-dealing, an uncertain future. At the moment, the crime level has gone down, which no doubt has to do with the security crew hired by the new investors. There it is, that emotionally weighted word: investor. Emblematic of so many places in this city, the RAW grounds' alternative culture is also somewhat defenceless before its two adversaries: the selfie-taking, binge-drinking, easyJet-tourism crowd on the one hand and the investors and gentrifiers on the other. Here they all come together, though it should be added that in this case it doesn't have to come to a horrible, tearful showdown. The current owner intends to build on part of the grounds, that much is clear – the unconventional character of the area, however, is to be protected, they say. It's possible that the investors might show sympathy for the colourful hustle and bustle. Or they are clever enough to realise that the continued existence of the RAW institutions can go hand in hand with economic interests, as a huge number of Berliners and tourists alike find this the place to be regardless of the season. Until the day, that is, that someone makes the crucial mistake and kills the whole thing through renovation.

What is clear, however, is that the residents and the people behind all the alternative projects sooner or later will have to bite some kind of bullet; the important thing is that the majority of projects can continue. And that the achievements of the alternative cultural scene that got the whole thing going will not simply degenerate into some kind of backdrop – but only the next couple of years will tell. Until that point people will party and drink, sing and buy things, protest and dance, struggle, haggle, and cheer.

Marzahn

An Unexpected Idyll Not Far from Concrete Blocks

HABERMANNSEE
KAULSDORFER SEEN
12621 BERLIN

'There's a trick,' my first teacher, Frau Werle, said, 'to drawing swans. Begin with the number two, then you already have the shape.' She was right. For a time, with great excitement, I almost only drew swans, just like in the previous phase I had almost only painted octopuses and in the phase before that Chinese women, all of whom wore big, triangular hats behind which there was a long plait; I knew that much from carnival.

Now it was swans. Majestic animals, they were never dirty, and they had friendly faces and loved their children, although those looked dishevelled and grey. Whenever I'd go on walks with my grandmother, we'd bring old

bread with us, tossing it to them off a small bridge, in the process angering the ducks, who were more agile and quicker than the big heroic swans, but had too much respect to try and snatch anything from them. In any event, that was true of me as well, for a girl in another class had told me she'd been attacked by a swan and almost swallowed alive. Apparently there had been an eyewitness, but I already believed it just like that. After all, I knew from *The Little Prince* that a snake could swallow an elephant in one go; there was even a drawing of it.

When some years ago I bought a used desk chair that had to be picked up in Kaulsdorf, I found myself chugging through that up-until-then unfamiliar area only to unexpectedly and surprisingly run into a medium-sized lake surround by reeds, leaves, and conifers: an entire biotope just a stone's throw from all of Marzahn's prefab high-rises. It was still early, and no one else seemed to have thought to seek out this place where the morning sun had chosen to shine its light. No one but a family of swans which understood themselves to be the sole proprietors of the lake and made it unmistakably clear to my curious dog to please not give them any more attention. The warning was loud, *ffff-chhhhhhhhh*, the performance dramatic, especially as a swan's wingspan can be more than two metres. We both took a step back at the same time and continued our walk around the enchanting lake.

Like its nearby siblings of Elsensee and Butzer See, the Habermannsee Lake was created when its gravel and sand were cleared to provide the material required to construct the new neighbourhoods of Hellersdorf and Marzahn in the 1940s. Groundwater and rain came together to form a happy alliance in the immense pits, and presto: the lakes (which, by the way, are of drinkable quality). Eels, pikes, and roach fish swim here throughout the year, and during the summer there is a mostly manageable collection of people who thankfully treat this place responsibly and take their rubbish away with them when they leave. An ideal model for the city and its multiple lakes. And parks. And just in general.

Cultural Centre with an Educational Mission and Tasty Cake

On the whole I'm pretty organised. Regrettably, this does not apply to all my paperwork: documents, bills, or receipts. When my yearly tax return comes around, for days my apartment looks like someone has turned everything upside down looking for some incriminating bits of microfilm. Pieces of paper everywhere, books on the floor, open drawers. Year after year, my accountant, Frau Strengmann, demands certain bills that I definitely never received. 'Yes, Frau Rust,' she says, 'you must have them.' I counter, 'I don't.' She replies, 'You most certainly do.' Hours later I'll send her a scan: 'Do you mean this here?' and she'll reply, 'That's what I said.'

BIESDORF PALACE AND ZKR-CENTRE FOR
ART AND PUBLIC SPACE
ALT-BIESDORF 55
12683 BERLIN
WWW.ZKR-BERLIN.DE

It's like a play we've been performing for many years, with the same dialogue and without any audience. Then I pack up all my junk in a large bag and set off on the long way to see her in Jotwede, leaving the city behind to make my way to the end of the world. I like Frau Strengmann a lot, but the way to her office makes me feel a bit gloomy. There is just this one endlessly long road out of the city, 20 minutes of unswerving road straight east, on either side only outlets, car dealerships, furniture discounters, and mattress stores. One day, as I had my dog with me, I decided to take one of the narrow side roads so that she could get a bit of air. I parked the car, got

out, and walked past a few houses to a park full of tall trees past which I could see all the way to a stately rose-coloured old villa. I later learned it was Biesdorf Palace. This is where the Siemens family once lived, and they were also responsible for the park, before everything went into the hands of the city at the end of the 1920s. In the 1950s, the two-storey villa functioned as a cultural centre for the municipality. More than half a century later, it hosts events once more, as Biesdorf Palace is now home to the Centre for Art and Public Space (ZKR). Its changing exhibitions are dedicated to international contemporary art. One of the ZKR's key areas of focus, however, is on the past, particularly on parallels and possible connections to art in the GDR. On their website, various figures from the worlds of art and culture describe the programme a bit loftily and, in my opinion, a bit too abstractly. Phrases like 'the construction of social discourses' from the 'arrangement of public space in relation to urban development' and so on. In spite of these circumlocutions, I became curious and returned to have a look at a photo exhibition.

I arrived here after a chance turn onto an unfamiliar side street. Once I was there, a sweet smell from the inside of the building drew me in, for the café offers excellent homemade cake. So I sat down on the veranda with a cup of coffee, gazed at the sculptures in the park, and sent Frau Strengmann an SMS to say I would be half an hour late. 'Traffic stress?' she asked. 'No,' I wrote back. 'On the contrary. I'm incredibly relaxed.'

Oberschöne-
weide

Concerts, Fairs, and GDR History

FUNKHAUS NALEPASTRASSE
NALEPASTRASSE 18
12459 BERLIN
TEL. 030 120 85 416
WWW.FUNKHAUS-BERLIN.DE

MILCHBAR IM FUNKHAUS
MON. - FRI. 10AM - 7PM,
SAT. - SUN. 11AM - 6PM

TIP

IF YOU'RE INTERESTED IN LEARNING MORE
ABOUT THE HISTORY OF THE FUNKHAUS
BEFORE AND AFTER THE FALL OF THE WALL,
YOU CAN TAKE A TOUR.

€ 15, INFO@DDR-FUNKHAUSTOUR.DE

The words ground loop, total harmonic distortion, and stereophonic sound all come from the realm of acoustics. Technical terms are great, especially for those on the outside. I got the idea to delve into the vocabulary of acoustics while reading about Berlin's Funkhaus and I came across the term flutter echo. Apparently flutter echo is exactly what you *don't* get in these studios near Oberschöneweide, and they are rightly proud of the fact. It's true, the former GDR radio-broadcasting premises still house one of the most renowned recording studios in the world.

If you make it out to the huge grounds off Nalepastrasse, you'll come encounter a cluster of buildings right on the side of the Spree, traversed by a number of paths between small patches of grass and tall old trees. The whole complex was built at the beginning of the 1950s upon the ruins of a partially destroyed veneer factory. Constituting one of the most unusual structures of the whole GDR regime, it is, in parts, listed. The architect and graphic designer responsible, Franz Ehrlich, was a Bauhaus student who spent some time working in the office of architect Walter Gropius. The conceptual and aesthetic influence of that era is impossible to ignore in the Funkhaus. The four main buildings currently feature concert halls, recording studios, event spaces, and artists' studios.

From 1951 to 1990, all the GDR's national radio programmes were produced and broadcast from here. The place was held to be a peer of West-German radio, and the almost 5000 people who worked here until the fall of the Wall helped make it possible. They produced radio plays and recorded albums of a quality that, among sound engineers and musicians, is considered unique. With its legendary acoustics, the large broadcast hall on the upper floor is the crowning jewel of the whole installation, and the list of international artists and orchestras that have recorded here is long, and runs from Depeche Mode and Sting all the way to conductors Daniel Barenboim and Kent Nagano, both of whom consider it the perfect place to record operas and symphonies.

In 2015, the complex changed hands. The new owner's idea is to keep the focus on high-quality music productions while having the grounds host more and more fairs (for example, a vegan food fair), conventions, and concerts. Gastronomy has long played a part too: amidst the mid-century designed rooms you will find the Milchbar, which offers lunch and a changing menu.

Lübars

56

BUS X21 QUICKBORNER STRASSE, BUS 222 ZABEL-KRÜGER-DAMM

Horses, Fields, Fresh Air

ALTER DORFKRUG
ALT-LÜBARS 8
13469 BERLIN
TEL. 030 922 10 230
THU. - SUN. 12PM - 9PM

KRÄUTERHOF LÜBARS
BERLINER WORKSHOPS FOR PEOPLE
WITH DISABILITIES
ALT-LÜBARS 15
13469 BERLIN
TEL. 030 390 960
MON. - THU. 10AM - 3PM,
FRI. 10AM - 12.30PM

My friend Lizzy didn't want to leave the city. 'I love Berlin. Out in the country I'll just fade away.' Lutz, on the other hand, whose name alliterates beautifully with his partner's, threatened to explode if they didn't escape to the country: 'If I have to deal with this traffic any longer, I'm going to freak out.' Lutz and Lizzy. A perfect couple. But as far as this topic was concerned, there didn't seem to be any agreement, and what's worse: like two tectonic plates they grew further and further apart from month to month, and you didn't want to imagine what would happen if they didn't find a solution. Friends gifted them wellness weekends and dance courses. Nothing helped.

When the back and forth threatened to grow into a real conflict, they took their child out of the line of fire for the summer and brought her to some friends of theirs who had a daughter the same age.

After three days, their daughter called. Her parents had counted on homesickness but were just asked to get her dusty riding clothes out of the cellar and bring them by as soon as possible. They got in the car and drove off. The northern-most part of Berlin, Lübars has one foot on the border of rural Brandenburg, yet it is no more than 25 minutes away from bustling Mitte or Charlottenburg. The road took them through parts of the city that Lutz found 'awful, just awful', streets full of discounters, shabby kebab stands and gambling halls, strange apartment blocks; surely not the most thrilling area, even Lizzy agreed. Then the Märkische Viertel: prefab high-rises, a satellite town in Reinickendorf – this is where rapper Sido is from. 'Oh man, I'm slowly beginning to understand Lutz,' Lizzy thought. Then from one second to the next, as if out of nowhere, a change of scenery that couldn't be any more surprising. To the left, concrete; to the right, wide fields, meadows, old houses, horses. Lübars. And that's where they ended up moving with their daughter, by the way. It was the best compromise they could make, a real gift, since you don't have to go far to be back in the big city. And if you want nature, you're in the right spot. The 18ᵗʰ-century village church is like a historical exclamation mark. There is an amusement park, a number of paddocks, a public swimming pool, and a children's farm. The Alte Dorfkrug tavern looks exactly like an old tavern ought to, with a terrace, beer garden, and big banquet hall. The first time I came to visit I thought that any minute my head would smack the glass dome they must have put over this place to protect and conserve it, but it never happened. Who knows how they manage to keep the village character of this place? They're successful. If you already live out in the country, you don't need to rush to visit Lübars. But anyone wanting to become more familiar with the contrasts of Berlin should come have a look. After a long walk through the fens there'll be a nice piece of fresh cake waiting at the Dorfkrug. Because this, too, is Berlin.

All across
Town

57

Dr Fish:
Trout-Whisperer

The day I decided I was going to move to Berlin was sunny and warm. My old friend Jörg, who I was staying with, suggested we go and eat breakfast at the market. The city and I had already been having an affair for some time, but the fact that we would have a shared future together was decided then. Walking down Winterfeldtstrasse – the hustle and bustle around the square, all the people sitting in the cafés, biting into their croissants, reading the paper, or talking with one another, passers-by carrying huge bouquets ... everywhere the smell of crêpes, Bratwurst, and fresh fish – it all became clear. This is where I wanted to live. Three weeks later, I moved.

JÜRGEN FÜRGUT
WED. 10AM – 2PM WINTERFELDTPLATZ
THU. 12PM – 5PM BRESLAUER PLATZ
FRI. 12PM – 7 PM ARKONAPLATZ
SAT. 10AM – 4PM WINTERFELDTPLATZ
WWW.STECKERFISCH.COM

In general, markets give off a special air. There are over 250 weekly markets in Berlin alone, and I would imagine that almost all of them sell great (organic) groceries and flowers. One of my favourites remains the Winterfeldtplatz market, which takes place on Saturdays (the large edition) and Wednesdays (the smaller version; very small in icy winter). I have a few favourite stands there, among others, Ergün, the friendliest cheese merchant in the world, whose selection is not only exquisite – you can also sample it immediately. I can quite unabashedly call him my dealer, as a constant craving for cheese is also an addiction. Ask him about the Heartbreaker or the Red Devil cheeses. You'll understand what I mean.

And then my man Dr Fish is there too, though I'm the only one who calls him that; his name is actually Jürgen, and his stand is called Steckerlfisch. Whatever the weather, he's always in a good mood there beneath his red pavilion, and he loves to grill his fresh mackerel, octopus, sea bream, sea bass, and rainbow trout. In addition to the fish, there are small sides like fresh bread and homemade potato salad. Jürgen comes from a small village southwest of Munich, at the edge of Lake Ammer, which is where he used to fish as a boy. At fourteen he got his fishing license, then came to study landscaping in Berlin. Though he originally planned to leave again after four years, by now he has happily been here for over twenty, with his wife and children. How do landscaping and fish come together? 'Listen, it's not like you imagine: a little flower here, a little tree there. It was really a lot of work, all elbows and little lies. No, Bettina, that's not who I am. As a foreman you have to lie all the time. Where your people are, when the site will be finished... I didn't know any more: was I lying to myself? Then I said to my wife: "Listen, if I keep on doing this, in two years I'm going to be retired, but with my jacket on the other way round." No joke.' In 2007, he went freelance, aged 35: 'On April 1. And you know what? I like it just as much as I did the very first day.'

You can see it. This man is a unique performer at the grill, his goods are tasty and fresh, excellent value for money. And this tip frees me from the heavy load of having to recommend just one market to you, since you can also find Steckerlfisch on Thursdays at Breslauer Platz and Fridays at Arkonaplatz.

58

Flea Markets: When Finders Become Keepers

WILMERSDORF:
MECKLENBURGISCHE STRASSE 32
14197 BERLIN
SUN. 8AM - 4PM

TIERGARTEN: STRASSE DES 17. JUNI
10623 BERLIN
SAT. - SUN. 10AM - 5PM

PRENZLAUER BERG: ARKONAPLATZ
10435 BERLIN
SUN. 10AM - 4PM

FRIEDRICHSHAIN: BOXHAGENER PLATZ
10245 BERLIN
SUN. 10AM - 6PM

SCHÖNEBERG: JOHN-F.-KENNEDY-PLATZ
10825 BERLIN
SAT. - SUN. 8AM - 4PM

When I was five or six, I first accompanied my mother to a flea market. She was interested in an art poster and haggled with the seller for so long that I sank into the ground with shame. But a few hours later, the poster was hanging in our hallway. I felt so sorry for the seller. How could my mother so assertively suggest a different price to him? You couldn't get away with that at the supermarket.

Not everyone can haggle. I will never become a haggler, but I am a dyed-in-the-wool flea-market-goer to this very day. The things I have dragged home with me over the years could fill a whole row of high-rises. Vases, sweaters, chairs, lamps: I like the

idea of recycling. You don't want it any more? Give it to me, it'll have a new home. And I like that the objects already have a past, even if I will never learn what it was. Furthermore, flea markets are the best places to study other people's lives. Why did someone collect owl pins for decades? Did they use them, or did they just lie around in some little box? And why, after thirty years of collecting and searching, did they one day just say: 'Right, that's it, people. I can't stand to look at any more owl pins. I'm taking the fifty I have here to the flea market.'? Fascinating. Books are another evocative sociogram. The person selling *Happy Over 50, Happy without Sugar*, and *Happiness –*

What is it? – maybe they've figured it out. Maybe they've given up looking for happiness and are now just patiently waiting for it to find *them*. You could always ask. With flea-market conversations you can theoretically come into contact with everything on the wide spectrum between Freud and daytime television. If you're interested, that is.

If you want to play it safe and you like things with a bit more taste, visit the alpha dog amongst flea markets on Strasse des 17. Juni. Most of the people selling things there are dealers, and the things themselves are generally not cheap, but often pretty and unusual. Here it has less to do with seeking than with finding. During the summer I often visit the flea market on Mecklenburgischen Strasse, which is primarily made up of private individuals and families who have come to sell their things, and you can tell that the objects come from well-to-do households.

The average sellers and buyers at my regular flea market, the one at the Schöneberger Rathaus, are more chaotic and a bit younger. Wait, is that where Kennedy once...? Indeed. In June 1963, John F. Kennedy visited Berlin, stood onto the balcony of the Rathaus, hungry and a bit hypoglycaemic from all the travelling, and said: *'Ick will oin Berliner'* (I want a Berliner, meaning a cream-filled donut), which later was modified a tad in all the history books. Weekend after weekend this historic location hosts a few good sellers and a few strange ones with knick-knacks and trinkets heaped in moving boxes, but the majority of the stands are rented by families or groups of friends who finally want to get rid of their mountains of clothes and household items. As many of the stands are covered, you can also visit this flea market when the weather's bad, even if it's not so busy. Which for a bargain-hunter is ideal anyway.

If you're traipsing around the east, do have a look at the flea markets on Arkonaplatz or Boxhagener Platz. Because both of them are in the middle of their respective neighbourhoods, you can even enjoy yourself before *and* after your visit to the flea market, for instance with breakfast and lunch. There are certainly enough cafés around both markets – something that is not necessarily the case with the aforementioned other flea markets.

59

Boat Tour: The Gentlest Way to Glide through Berlin

HOP ON AND OFF ALMOST EVERYWHERE IN BERLIN. FOR ADDRESSES, DEPARTURE TIMES, AND LENGTH OF TRIPS, SEE THE RESPECTIVE COMPANIES' WEBSITES:

REEDEREI RIEDEL
WWW.REEDEREI-RIEDEL.DE

REEDEREI BRUNO WINKLER
WWW.REEDEREIWINKLER.DE

STERN UND KREISSCHIFFAHRT
WWW.STERNUNDKRIES.DE

The river Spree and I, we've had some lovely experiences together. Once I was a guest at a party that was held on a small steamer. Sixty festive people attacked the buffet, emptied the bar, and whirled around the dancefloor that had been cleared of its tables and chairs, returning to the deck in order to let the endorphins of a wild evening evaporate into the night air through the now damp fabric of their dresses and shirts (big tour, 6 hours).

Another time I booked a tour through the government district (1 hour) to interview the famous chef and restaurant owner Sarah Wiener. Outside, the rain was coming down in buckets, so we turned out to be the only passengers on board: she, me, the camera team, and the little steamer crew. There was not a moment's pause to our talk. I can only recommend a trip during rainy weather. As Berlin silently and gently glided past our windows like a movie, the weather and grey light made the images look like they were in black and white, here and there pierced by a few colourful umbrellas and passers-by defiantly leaning into the wind. Protected on the boat, we bit into crispy sausages and shared the mustard while every glance outside revealed that the diligent stagehands had already changed the panorama again. I could tell a few more boat stories, but by and large they all say the same thing: if you would like to get to know this city or to deepen your relationship with it, you should definitely take advantage of Berlin's wonderful boats, ships, and steamers.

There are many providers and tours, ranging from short (1 hour), medium (2.5 hours), to long (4–6 hours plus dinner). Some have to be booked beforehand, others are 'hop on, hop off': just as with bus tours, you can get on and off at various stops or rather jetties. You can go from Berlin to Potsdam or even to the Spreewald, while at the same time – depending on the offer – booking tasty menus. Naturally, in good weather there is a lot happening on the Spree, that's when smaller boats meet the bigger ones, excursion steamers meet rowboats, and you wave or just let it go, depending on how many encounters you've already had. On some of the tours the guide is made of flesh and blood, while on others it comes in the form of earbuds. You just have to decide which programme you want. There are historical bridge tours and trips that highlight Berlin's history throughout various eras (while unmistakably making clear how truly annoying it is to have known so much of it yet already forgotten it all again; my kingdom for a good history teacher!) There are no-frills trips, tours with whisky tastings and crime-story readings, 'typical Berlin tours' with local stories, songs, and snacks, and so on and so on.

Once again: boat tours in bad weather can be wonderful, and it's not only seasoned melancholics who will agree. When the water below you meets the water above, and you're sitting in a glass capsule silently sliding through the city, past old and new, places decrepit and chic, you finally get the chance to at long last hear your own thoughts a little more clearly.

INDEX